Spirit of the Valley

Spirit of the Valley

Where the Light of Science
Meets the Shadow of Myth

Baxter Trautman

SIERRA CLUB BOOKS
San Francisco

The Sierra Club, founded in 1892 by John Muir, has devoted itself to the study and protection of the earth's scenic and ecological resources—mountains, wetlands, woodlands,
wild shores and rivers, deserts and plains. The publishing program of the Sierra Club
offers books to the public as a nonprofit educational service in the hope that they may
enlarge the public's understanding of the Club's basic concerns. The point of view
expressed in each book, however, does not necessarily represent that of the Club. The
Sierra Club has some sixty chapters coast to coast, in Canada, Hawaii, and Alaska. For
information about how you may participate in its programs to preserve wilderness and
the quality of life, please address inquiries to Sierra Club, 85 Second Street, San
Francisco, CA 94105.

www.Sierraclub.org/books

Published by Sierra Club Books, in conjunction with Crown Publishers, New York, New
York. Member of the Crown Publishing Group.
Random House, Inc., New York, Toronto, London, Sydney, Auckland
www.randomhouse.com

SIERRA CLUB, SIERRA CLUB BOOKS, and Sierra Club design logos are registered
trademarks of the Sierra Club.

Originally published by Black Mountain Press in 1998.

Printed in the United States of America on acid-free paper containing a minimum
of 50% recovered waste paper, of which at least 10% of the fiber content is post-
consumer waste.

Cover design by Mary Schuck
Book design by Troy Scott Parker/Cimarron Design

Typeset in Monotype Perpetua, designed by Eric Gill and released between 1925 and
1932. Acorn motif from the rare 1900 edition of the American Type Founders Cut Book.

Library of Congress Cataloging-in-Publication Data
Trautman, Baxter. Spirit of the valley / by Baxter Trautman
Includes bibliographical references. (alk. paper)
1. Natural History — California — San Luis Obispo County. 2. Savanna ecology —
California — San Luis Obispo County. 3. Oak — Ecology — California — San Luis
Obispo County. 4. Nature — Folklore. I. Title.
QH105.C2 T73 2000
508.794'78 — dc21 00-029143
ISBN 1-57805-061-8

First Sierra Club Edition

For
Mrs. Bunny Binewski
and
all the four-legged Muses

Table of Contents

List of Figures

Prologue

This book is an invitation to the unconventional wedding of science and mythology. As in any good marriage the partners compliment each other's strengths and weaknesses, and so it is with the marriage of science and mythology. One is mostly mind, the other mostly heart.

As a poet, I am continually frustrated by dull accumulations of biological statistics and data that seem to have no relation to the living landscape they describe. But then as a scientist, I am often appalled by my own ignorance of the precise workings of my environment. The scientist in me is fascinated by the finite details of how an organism works, like the specific construction of a woodpecker's skull, which can absorb blows that would kill a human being. Or a bluebird's feathers. How can they be blue yet hold no blue pigments?

My other personality, the poet, cherishes the sprawling, romantic mythologies around these organisms. For example, why is the woodpecker family named after a long-forgotten Greek prince, or why do bluebirds, of all the birds in the world, symbolize happiness? My poet sees a part of the landscape and ties it to broad, cultural continuums of mythology, history and art. Seeing the same thing, my scientist wants to pull it apart and see how it works.

Within these pages are organisms commonly found in central coast oak savanna communities. These are communities dominated by valley oaks and an understory of grasses. Blue oaks, interior live oaks, and digger pines share the landscape as well. Each part of the landscape mentioned herein, be it an oak tree, fence lizard, or native grass, is represented from the perspective of both a poet and a scientist. Uniting science and mythology brings soul to the former and rationality to the latter. Together they make a whole and enduring partnership.

The Valley

The fishing town I live in on the coast of central California is cool and gray at this time of year. The fog billows in off the Pacific Ocean at the end of spring and seems to stay the entire summer. It will drift reluctantly back to sea for a few hours every afternoon then around sunset it rushes vengefully back to land. In this damp miasma mildew accumulates on everything, seemingly even the pores of my skin. I am unable to see the morning or nighttime sky for weeks at a time and my spirits hang like the shroud of fog. After weeks of this I load my truck with books and food, and flee to the yellow heat of the interior valleys.

A favorite destination is a narrow valley branching off from the great Salinas Valley to stretch northeast from San Luis Obispo County into Monterey County. A thin strip of road winds steadily past handsome horse farms and humble, decaying ranches whose glory days (if they ever had any) are now a gauzy memory. All the land is privately owned in the valley and cruci-fied oaks silently warn against hunting or trespassing.

We roll along, the dog and I, windows down and hair ruffled, both of us smelling the warm, dusty air. The road bisects broad fields of grass freckled with oaks. My spirits rise and I imagine the mildew recoiling like the Wicked Witch when Dorothy con-fronted her with a pail of water. We have escaped the clammy grasp of the fog and entered into the warm, strong, arms of the sun.

Miles down the road I roll the truck under the broad canopy of a live oak. Mick jumps out of the truck and immediately establishes his territory. I sit on the tailgate like a sponge in a giant puddle of heat and silence.

Lao-Tzu noted centuries ago that "the spirit of the valley never dies...use it and you will never wear it out."[1] Over the coming days I am to make much use of this advice.

California

AN OLD NAVAJO GENTLEMAN once explained to me that his people have three dawns to their day. First dawn is a vague grayness that penetrates the black, signaling that the reign of the night is over. Second dawn is that shape-shifting, indefinable period between the dissolving of the grayness and the emergence of the new sun. Once the sun itself becomes visible it is third dawn.

I awoke in the middle of the second dawn and was able to say "see you tonight" to some of the stars. Mick and I stretched and he wagged his sleepy, happy tail then we went for a walk down the road. Mick's luck is good this morning. Breakfast was a hastily crunched and gulped ground squirrel. I'd like to say he was agile enough to have caught it himself but it was already dead in the center of the road. Now, adroit cottontails lead him on fruitless chases around the field. I am content with more sedentary pursuits and watch a large flock of bluebirds at the cattle trough. The cattle dissipated into the hills during the night and I see where they are hulked down under the trees working on their cud. Mick huffs and puffs into the hollow end of a fallen tree and I lean crossed forearms against a fence post dotted white with bird droppings. The day is warm and the sun's not even over the horizon yet. The stillness and incipient heat conspire to make me daydream. In the somnolence of the early morning my mind slips its moorings to the present and drifts lazily back in time. I imagine I can hear a rag-tag band of Spanish soldiers passing through this valley. Their mules are thin, a few ride bony horses, but most of the men walk. They are unwashed and unshaven, deeply tan from the California sun they have been cursing.

They call this land California in the tradition of their kinsmen who sailed the coast of Baja California in the 16th century. During these earlier explorations a novel by Garcia Ordoñez de Montalvo was being widely read back home.[1] *The Exploits of Esplandian* included a battle against a certain Queen Califa, ruler of an island near the Indies. On this island was a rugged, mountain-ringed valley of infernal heat named California, from *calida*, meaning "hot," and *fornax*, meaning "furnace." The first Spaniards must have been here in the summer for the name fit. If today is as typical as the rest of this July week has been then the temperature will easily rise to 110 degrees Fahrenheit by early afternoon.

This hellish land Montalvo described was occupied by a fierce race of black women very much like the fabled Brazilian Amazons. With their weapons of shining gold these women would capture men in battle and drag them home to keep as captive breeding stock. Trained griffins taken at birth from their caves were kept nearby (curiously like the California Condor chicks captured from their caves by local Native Americans) and when the hapless males were finished with their reproductive duties they were tossed to the hungry creatures.[2]

After crushing and looting the Aztec empire the Spaniards were especially keen on finding a mythical land farther north. In one of his official reports to the King in 1524 Cortés spoke confidently of finding an island rich in gold and pearls, populated entirely by women, and just a ten-day journey from his location in Mexico.[3] Worse, however, than running into a band of griffin-bearing Amazons, Cortés ran head-on into the wrath of King Charles waiting impatiently in Spain for Cortés to return laden with riches. Fearing his explorer was trying to create his own kingdom far from Charles' reach, the king put Cortés on a short leash.[4] Meanwhile, other Spanish explorers searched for the fabled paradise they were sure lay north of the newly conquered Mexican territories.

It seems that dreamers have consistently looked to California for their Eden. The Spaniards were searching for unlimited gold, the fountain of youth, and a water passage across the continent. They were followed centuries later by men from the eastern side of the country who were still looking for gold. Decades later more Easterners would come but this time the gold they sought was in the form of celluloid, and millions of people sought their end of the rainbow in Hollywood.

And still they keep coming. Why shouldn't they, for in a sense California *is* an Eden. With greater geographical, biological and climatic diversity than any other continental American state, California can also lay claim to the greatest number of endemic species, species found nowhere else on the planet.[5] California stretches roughly 800 miles up and down the Pacific Coast of North America. It encompasses 10 degrees of latitude and a wealth of influential topography. These associations combine to produce highly variable climates favorable for a wide variety of organisms, including *Homo sapiens*. From the temperate rain forests of northern California down to the semi-deserts of the south, there is something here for everyone. That must be paradise.

Biophilia

ICK AND I LEAVE THE BIRDS and rabbits and wander back to the truck. I perk a cup of coffee on the tailgate, marveling as I do so at the force of habit that makes me do this even though the temperature is already well into the eighties.

I balance the coffee on a stack of books and settle into the shade of the live oak we're parked next to. Thumbing through a journal from William H. Brewer I find the following excerpt:

> APRIL 29, 1861—On passing the Santa Lucia [mountain range] the entire aspect of the country changed. It was as if we had passed into another land and another clime. The Salinas Valley thus far is much less verdant than we anticipated. There are more trees but less grass. Imagine a plain ten to twenty miles wide, cut up by valleys into innumerable hills from two to four hundred feet high, their summits of nearly the same level, their sides rounded into gentle slopes. The soil is already dry and parched, the grass already as dry as hay, except along streams, the hills brown as a stubble field. But scattered over these hills and in these valleys are trees every few rods—great oaks, often of immense size, ten, twelve, eighteen, and more feet in circumference, but not high; their wide-spreading branches making heads

often over a hundred feet in diameter—of the deepest green foliage—while from every branch hangs a trailing lichen, often several feet long and delicate as lace. In passing over this country, every hill and valley presents a new view of these trees—here a park, there a vista with the blue mountains ahead. I could never tire of watching some of these beautiful places of natural scenery.[1]

I look up at the great oaks in the valley before me. I know exactly what Brewer meant. There's a meditative quality to admiring a landscape. My eyes gather the features of the land and my body absorbs the view at a microscopic level. Every cell relaxes, floating in the fluid mirror of my gaze.

In this state of contentment I reach for a book from the stack beside me, *Biophilia* by Harvard biologist Dr. Edward O. Wilson.[2] In 1984 Wilson postulated the controversial theory that human beings are instinctively drawn to other living organisms, and that our survival as a species depends upon this inborn curiosity. Wilson called this theory the biophilia hypothesis, *bio* standing for "living things," and the Greek *philia*, for a "tending toward." His theory postulates that humans are naturally drawn to other living organisms and that this biophilia is a result of our genetic evolution, that "genes and culture are held together by an elastic but unbreakable leash."[3]

Wilson might describe Brewer's and my feelings as a biophilic response to the vista. As humans evolved over thousands and thousands of years we had to learn which things in the environment were good and nurturing and which were dangerous or harmful. Survival depended on learning this information. According to Wilson this wisdom was acquired through an *inborn* and crucial curiosity about our surroundings.

Wilson and his colleague Charles Lumsden bravely proposed that genes and culture not only evolve together but in response to each other. This "gene-culture coevolution" is

a complicated, fascinating interaction in which culture is generated and shaped by biological imperatives while biological traits are simultaneously altered by genetic evolution in response to cultural innovation.[4]

Early in our evolutionary history this genetic drive molded human behavior towards an extreme awareness, and subsequent responsiveness, to the environment. Immobile objects and landscapes didn't take much observation, while on the other hand, ephemeral living organisms were far more apt to inspire attention and spur curiosity. Over time we learned to associate positive results with pleasurable or useful organisms while at the same time learned the negative results possible from dangerous organisms. As a result, recognition of a good thing in our environment is felt as a literal biophilia. This biophilia engenders feelings or physical sensations that are favorable or positive. We wish to associate with that object.

The opposite of biophilia would be biophobia, a "fear of living things" which causes us to avoid these objects.[5] Some of our most common phobias are of snakes, spiders, heights, closed spaces, and blood. If humans did indeed evolve in the darkest heart of Africa, descending from the jungle trees on all fours to take our place on two feet in the broad sweeping savannas, imagine the terrors of the trial and error involved in that ancient evolutionary process. Numerous snakes and spiders, many of them poisonous, inhabit the African forests. It would be a prudent evolutionary step to develop an aversion to these animals. Over time it would be a successful biological adaptation for us to have developed a genetic, or inborn fear of the dangerous things in our habitat.

Monkeys and apes instinctively react to snake-like objects with extreme agitation.[6,7] My dogs are certainly not as intelligent as primates yet they too show a strong aversion to snakes and even snake-like objects. Upon discovering a length of black rubber hosing coiled in the weeds by our driveway they barked at it for hours. The hose didn't move and eventually they quit woofing and circling around it. But for weeks until I relented and threw the hose away they continued to warily circumvent that side of the driveway.

On the other hand, doe-eyed animals, open spaces, sturdy shade trees, and flowers, tend to elicit a biophilic reaction like the one Brewer noted in his journal.[8] Usually these parts of the natural world are at least benign if not outright useful.

Furry, gentle-eyed herbivores have been a primary human food source for thousands of years, while for an equally long time flowers have presented a visual and olfactory cue that some sort of grain, fruit or nut would soon be forthcoming. Solid, well-built trees offer numerous advantages: respite from heat, in the form of shade, and respite from cold in the form of fuel for fires and building materials for shelters. In addition, they offer concealment while at the same time presenting a prime surveillance post. All this would make trees highly valued commodities as early human beings moved away from the confines of the forest and out into the open savannas.

Much testing has been done concerning landscape preferences in human beings and a frequent conclusion is that we prefer open, park-like spaces to forests or jungles.[9] (Note the use of the word "frequent." Enormous variables, such as age, health, culture, and gender tend to produce different responses as to what is a "preferred" habitat or landscape.) These preferences are probably related to the innate feelings of safety and security that these spaces provide. Here accidental encounters with predatory or harmful animals would be greatly reduced. Should these threats occur the chances of escaping them in a broad, tree-speckled savanna would be much higher than in a cramped and darkened forest.

As animals have aversions, so they have preferences. Most instinctively prefer particular spaces in a landscape. For instance, large, heavy raptors seek the easy accessibility of a tree top, while smaller birds tend to look for shelter within the tree's canopy. The even smaller birds frequently associate with areas of very dense vegetative cover. Each type of bird is biologically programmed to seek the part of the environment which is most hospitable to them.

Every culture has stories which incorporate the plants and animals in their environment. This acknowledgment is part of the power of biophilia. For all but the last few centuries of human development, the recognition of these organisms was crucial in our relationship to a world we were much more intimately connected to. For industrialized nations, this need to recognize components of the landscape has been lost. The dangers we need to be aware of today are drive-by shooters, muggers, and strangers offering us candy. Very few of us regularly encounter venomous insects and vipers, and even more rarely do we round a corner and come face to face with wolves, bears or very large and long-toothed cats.

Elizabeth Lawrence writes in *The Biophilia Hypothesis* that "for a large share of the industrialized world, relationships with animals as they are symbolically perceived have to a great extent replaced interactions with their living counterparts."[10] The danger in this symbolical perception is that long after many plants and animals have lost their power to harm or help humans we still perceive them as either good or bad and frequently contribute to their existence based on these obsolete values.

Deer, for example, are usually symbolized as "good" animals. Their numbers and existence are encouraged. I have seen hunters who take better care of a wild deer herd than they do their own dogs. Deer meat is a valuable commodity. I also know suburban gardeners who will spend hundreds of dollars to keep deer out of their flower beds but who wouldn't dream of hurting one. They wish the deer wouldn't eat their flowers but they *like* having them around.

Large, dangerous predators, however, are often seen as "bad" animals. To the hunter, a mountain lion reduces the amount of game available. To the flower gardener, mountain lions eat animals perceived as "Bambi" and have the potential to eat "Fido" and "Fluffy" as well. In addition, the mountain lion can cause great personal and bodily harm to both the gardener and the hunter. Based on these perceptions it becomes sensible to kill mountain lions. They become unnecessary in the overall scheme of things. Hunters will eagerly take over their role in controlling deer numbers and the gardeners might even feel a little more secure when their backs are turned to the dark and uncultivated peripheries of their property.

In our ancient past there were good reasons for human beings to reject, separate, and isolate ourselves from various parts of the environment while encouraging or worshipping other parts. This was a vision understandable to a people in daily contact with an environment capable of both nurturing and devastating. It would be logical to assign a "good" and "bad" status to all the aspects encountered in one's world. But our daily environment has changed dramatically. In speaking of landscape preferences J. Appleton says we are,

> living in a very different world from that of the primitive man whose very survival depended on that ability to see without being seen...The removal of urgent necessity does not put an end to the machinery which evolved to cope with it.[11]

As result of perceptions stemming from innate biological reflexes (and encouraged by mythologies) modern humans continue to react to the natural world in ways that may not ultimately be to our best advantage. This behavior is not wrong, merely obsolete.

This is a vital time in our evolution to admit that there may indeed be "an elastic but unbreakable leash" between our genes and our culture. We need to gaze bravely at the idea that much of human behavior could be motivated by biological imperatives. Only by recognizing this process can we begin to alter indiscriminate behaviors and responses to the world, responses which had their place as mankind evolved in steppe and forest, but which may be dangerously outdated and unnecessary for town and city.

Steinbeck

M Y COFFEE WAS GOOD but it's all gone, and now it's too hot to make more. Besides, the coffee did its job: not to wake me up, for it's only decaffeinated, but to reassure me that all is right in my world.

The little motions of making the coffee—pouring the water, measuring the grinds, waiting for it to perk, the smell of it, the minuscule vapors as I pour it—all this ritual symbolizes that the pace and order of my day is proceeding uninterrupted and unchanged. If I have time enough to make and enjoy coffee, then there is no chaos, no calamity. That might come later, but right now all is serene. Coffee drinking in western culture evolved in casual and relaxed settings. I am the product of generations of coffee klatches, coffee breaks, and cafes, and I lazily wonder if my affinity for this drink stems from a biophilic response.

I put Dr. Wilson away and pick up John Steinbeck. I fell asleep last night with this tattered copy of *To a God Unknown* resting on my chest. Steinbeck incorporated some of the worlds greatest mythologies into his works, and in this novel he works with the ancient pagan themes of sacrifice and renewal.[1] This was Steinbeck's third novel and the critics panned it yet it remains my favorite. I return over and over to the character of

Joseph Wayne, a man so possessed by the spirit of the land that he eventually sacrifices himself to it.

Wayne is an eastern transplant who falls in love with the lush California grasses and deep-shaded oak trees. Steinbeck set the novel in a valley west of the Salinas River, in a valley much like this one. When I read that Wayne built his house under a giant oak tree I know Steinbeck was picturing a towering, thick-trunked valley oak like the ones in this valley.

In preparation for his ultimate sacrifice Wayne travels to a somber grove on a ridge top that is guarded by "black pines." Encircled by the tall, oppressive pines, a massive dark rock dominates the middle of the hurst. Steinbeck consistently describes this eerie place as dark and separate from the open, rolling green countryside below. His choice of words to create this uncomfortable setting inadvertently lent credence to Wilson's biophilia hypothesis.

Looming over the western edge of the Salinas Valley are the Santa Lucia Mountains. I can see a length of its ridged back when I climb the hill behind me. Steinbeck grew up in view of these mountains and he often wrote of them with foreboding, hinting of ancient and threatening forces that lurked in the range's dark folds and canyons.[2] I climbed to the hilltop last night to catch as much as I could of the fading sun. As twilight blackened the Santa Lucias I felt a brief, creeping anxiety. The mountains *were* vaguely foreboding and for a moment I shared Steinbeck's unease.

In *East of Eden* he describes an inexplicable "dread of west," where "the night drifted back from the ridges of the Santa Lucias" and which came to represent for him the "death of the day."[3] I suspect most people have an instinctual fear of darkness. Was his fear a similar, innate response to centuries filled with fading suns and lightless nights, centuries in which human beings learned that darkness left them vulnerable in their environment?

In Wilson's book I read that for the greater part of their history people lived in consummate and wholly interdependent relationships with the landscape. He thought it "quite extraordinary…that all learning rules related to that world have been erased in a few thousand years."[4] Maybe Steinbeck and I felt the same anxious twinge because these "rules" are encoded in our blood. Our genes overrode the conditioning of our rational minds, conditioning that chided "Don't be silly. There's no logical reason to fear these mountains, they're just sharp rock and ground." That voice is loud, but our blood knows better. Our blood listens to what our minds won't hear.

Despite my fleeting anxiety as darkness closed over the landscape I also felt comfort in knowing that Steinbeck felt the same way. I sat hugging my knees and though I was alone, for a moment I felt a shivery kinship to this man. The mountains gave me a relationship with another human being, to a person no longer living yet not dead. People only truly, finally die when there is no one who remembers them.

An unknown man and the mountains are just one example of many long and stretching connections to this world. It is a world of great time and mystery, of which I am but a small part. This is a fine and generous thought that, one that smoothes the ragged edges of a frenetic existence. As I write this I stop for a moment and gaze around. Whatever I look at—an oak tree, a pale moon weak in the light of day, a blue sky—arouses a sense of connection within me: to a man who grew up in a valley studded with these very same oaks; to the same moon my kin will stare at when all that remains of me are a handful of faded photographs; to the same blue sky shining all over the world at some time today. The landscape continually tethers me to past, present and future worlds. These iron tethers bind me to the earth, yet the security of their grip enables me to soar unfettered. When I remember that I am related to people who have passed and to people who have yet to be I become a part of something far greater and much larger than my own life. There is an ease and comfort in this continuity.

I am alone but I am not lonely. Ghosts comfort me everywhere I look. Indeed, upon his arrival in the valley Joseph

Wayne knew "that this land is full of ghosts." [5] That is another memory that Steinbeck and I hold in our blood.

FOUR

Annual Grasses

EVER AT MY SIDE, Mick looks up expectantly as I stretch against the languid air.

"Come here, buddy," and he does. I rub his ears and pull a stray foxtail off his tawny coat. On our way over here yesterday we stopped at the veterinarian's office and limped away an hour and $125 later. Seems just such a foxtail had worked its way between the webbing of his paw to the other side of his foot. This isn't a new thing. Every summer the animals start getting them stuck in their ears and feet and every summer I hear horror stories as I sit in the vet's office, about how they worked into the spine of one woman's cat, into the heart of anothers dog. We all shake our heads in commiseration.

Mick, I suspect, though I will never know for sure, is half Golden Retriever and half Golden Labrador. His coat is long like a retriever's and he has absolutely no business roaming through the weeds with me for he is soon sporting any number of awns, burrs and bristles. Foxtails are what I generically call most of these furtive hitchhikers, but a wide variety of species utilize Mick's generous and unwitting taxi service. The plants that cause him the greatest misery are the wild barleys and the ripgut grasses, species of the genus *Hordeum* and *Bromus* which ripple on the hillsides in summer like a calm tan sea. In the spring each shoot will sprout a bushy head of seeds housed in botanically complicated packages called spikelets. As tender green shoots and seeds both the barleys and the grasses provide good forage for grazing animals. As spring wears on, the long and bristly arms of the spikelets dry up, becoming hard and brittle. This is when they prove so injurious to grazing animals and passing pets. After seeing how it affected animals that had eaten it, ranchers gave the ripgut brome (*Bromus rigidus*) its gruesome name.

Each spikelet carries a seed encased in bristly sheaths.[1] These sheaths, called glumes, are evolutionary marvels. Designed to protect and disseminate their individual seeds, the glumes carry out their mission with an efficiency that would leave most parents feeling a dejected inadequacy. First the glumes protect their little seeds from the elements by encasing them. Their barbed bristles also protect them from predators.

The barbs are layered on the outside of the glumes like a bunch of "v"s stacked into each other. When the pointed tip of the glume (the rachis) penetrates a surface, all the arms of the"v"s press up vertically against each other and offer no resistance to the entry. But if the glume is pulled backward all the "v" shaped bristles spread horizontally, offering tremendous resistance against whatever they have penetrated. Continued tugging on the spikelet results in the upper tips of the glume snapping off while the lower portion with its seed snuggled safely inside remains in its burrow. Hopefully at this point the burrow is a profitable patch of soil and not my jeans or Mick's foot, because the best way to completely remove the spikelets at this point is to grasp them at the rachis and pull them on through—awkward if I have to take my jeans off in the middle of a field or expensive if the vet has to operate.

Locomotion is also one of the glumes functions. Their tops culminate in a long, prickly structure called an awn. The velcro-like bristles on the extended awn will easily snag on a passing bird or mammal allowing the entire spikelet to be carried away from the parent plant. When the ferrying animal scratches or

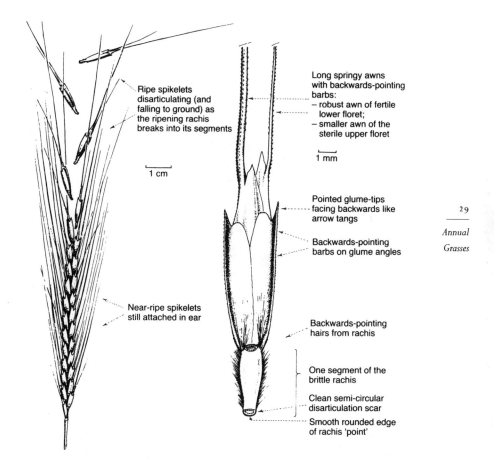

Fig. 1. Diagram of wheat spikelets and a single spikelet. (From *Grass Evolution and Domestication*. Copyright © 1992 by G.P. Chapman, Ed. Reprinted by permission of Cambridge University Press.)

grooms itself the hitchhiking spikelet is dislodged before it can burrow into the animal's flesh and cause serious damage. This is how the seed leaves its natal site. Distance from the birth place eliminates competition from parent and sibling plants and can allow a species to establish itself in an area where it might not exist already.

Having a foothold in many areas is genetically safer for most species. Imagine if I, an only child, had five children that all built their houses next to mine in Hordeum Holler. If a flood swept the town of Hordeum Holler away one day, our entire lineage would be gone. The population of Trautmans in Hordeum Holler would be extinct. If, however, one child moved down the road to Bromus Buttes, another went up the road to Awn Arbor, and a third lived across Glume Gulch, there would still be three Trautmans surviving in the area.

If I take a walk in the summer through any field, lot, or woodland, I inevitably wind up with the progeny of at least one *Hordeum* or *Bromus* in the crease of my boot or hem of my jeans. Sometimes these spikelets will be hundreds of miles from their birthplace and amazingly, they can be traced back 10,000 years to their ancestral homes in the broad and ancient valleys of Iraq and Iran.[2]

More Annual Grasses

J UST AS THE VALLEYS of California are tremendously
fruitful, so are the valleys of Iraq and Iran. At roughly
the same 30-40 degree north latitudes, they share
rugged topographies and Mediterranean climates
characterized by hot, dry summers followed by cool,
wet winters.

I am puzzled when I hear these middle-eastern lands reviled,
for in this revilement all humanity denounces its heritage. In
these deep and darkly fertile valleys our ancestors literally cradled the seeds of our civilization by learning to take grain seed,
put it in the soil, and nurture it to maturity. Some seed from the
mature plants was kept to be replanted, some was eaten right
away, and most importantly, some was stored to be eaten later.
This allowed people to turn away from a capricious reliance on
hunting and gathering to concentrate instead on creating a sustainable, reliable food source. As they became more adept at
agriculture they began to focus on luxuries such as art and archi-
tecture. As a result, civilization emerged from these valleys.

Some of the seeds first harvested in the Middle Eastern valleys were from the wild wheats and barleys. These weeds produced numerous, fat seeds able to remain dormant through the
periodic droughts that plagued their homeland. These cherished
seeds became a significant source of complex carbohydrates and

proteins for the Sumerians and Babylonians. Although certain varieties were favored over others, the art of winnowing seed was imprecise at best and less desirable species ended up mixed in with the good. As the technique of agriculture spread from the Eastern valleys, both the good and bad seeds increased their ranges as well. By the year Christ was born, these grains were being planted in the neighboring arable regions of Western Europe and Northern Africa and no longer just for human consumption but for livestock as well.[1]

We know these seeds can travel with ease so it is only a short stretch to imagine how they migrated to the New World. Picture a Spanish bull grazing peaceably beneath an oak tree surrounded by tall, bowing weeds and grasses. Instead of being sent to the bullfights in Madrid, this bull is marched across the fields where he and a couple dozen head of cattle are boarded onto Spanish brigantines. The ships set sail for the islands of the Caribbean, their captains bent on obtaining treasures for the crown. In the holds below, the bull and his bovine companions contentedly munch the fodder collected for them from the wide and sunny Spanish plains, fodder that no doubt included various specimens of *Hordeum* and *Bromus* grasses. Quarters are cramped for the cattle. They stand and sleep in their fodder and as they do tenacious spikelets of *Hordeum* and *Bromus* find comfortable lodging on the cattle hides. Beef and fodder cross the ocean to Cuba, Hispaniola and other Antilles islands.

Upon their arrival the cattle are herded down the gangplank. The remaining fodder is tossed out into a wagon. For a few days the cattle are held in a corral near the port and fed the last of their food. Eventually they are released into selected fields to graze at will. The old fodder litter remains in the corral. A handful of *Hordeum* and *Bromus* seeds take root in the well-fertilized soil. Meanwhile, a few miles away a cow scratches against a sturdy tree and dislodges a ripgut spikelet from her coat. Another cow makes a cow pie and passes through an undigested barley seed. The seeds take root on the new islands.

In 1520 Cortés imports cattle and grain from these islands to the Aztec empires he is conquering in Mexico.[2] Cattle and seed flourish in their new home. Two-hundred forty-nine years later Captain Fernando de Rivera y Moncada provides overland support from Mexico for a sea journey to the bay of Monterey.[3] On this expedition he drives 200 head of cattle into San Diego where he rendezvous with the Spanish sea crew led by Captain Portola.[4] At last, the progeny of the bull from Madrid have made their way to California.

As the rest of the expedition heads north, the cattle remain behind with a handful of Jesuit priests who are left to found the mission of San Diego. To support themselves in this new land, the fathers raise cattle and wheat. Their mission thrives and eventually other missions are founded along the California coast.

Cattle and seed with origins in the Old World are brought to each of these missions. The tough Spanish cattle are well-adapted to the New World. So are the miscellaneous *Hordeum* and *Bromus* seeds inevitably associated with the high-quality wheat seed. Both flourish in the dry, Mediterranean-like climate to which they are well-accustomed.

As a result of time and travel, biology and topography, Mick has a hole in his paw and I have another $125 on my Visa card. Yet I find it humbling and at the same time comforting to look at this little wild barley spikelet laying in the palm of my hand. The long journey this little plant has taken over the course of centuries parallels my journey over the same period.

Just as this little seed is obviously not the same seed that was tilled in an Iraqi village 10,000 years ago, so I am not the same woman that was tending the seeds in the warm, sun-drenched soil of a Middle Eastern valley 10,000 years ago. Yet I am related to her. We come from the same source. Albeit we have evolved and diverged significantly from each other we still have more in common than we do not. Same bones, organs, reproductive patterns, same desires for food, shelter, and mates; just like these little seeds have the same built-in drives to sprout, take root, and reproduce like millions of seeds before them. And both of

us owe who we are today to the valleys that cradled and nour-
ished us and propelled us along the path that would wind
through centuries of days and nights, dust and rain, empires
built and lost.

Here we sit, together at last, the fates of seed and animal
inextricably bound through time. We are like the honeybee that
E. O. Wilson reflects upon in *Biophilia*:

> Through fossil remains in rock and amber, we know that its
> lineage goes back at least 50 million years. Its contemporary
> genes were assembled by an astronomical number of events
> that sorted and recombined the constituent nucleotides.
> The species evolved as the outcome of hourly contacts with
> thousands of other kinds of plants and animals along the
> way.[5]

I am staggered by the immense numbers of days and nights,
matings and reproductions that have passed just to get this seed
and me here. We have shared a long journey and both of us are
dwarfed in the colossal, implacable march of time. This seed and
I are but one brief step in a tremendously stretching journey; a
journey that started long before us and which will hopefully
continue long after we have broken down into our respective
components of carbon, hydrogen, oxygen and various other
elements.

With the humble recognition of our very small part in this
trip comes a deep sense of comfort, in that without me, without
this seed, the next steps in time's lengthy wanderings are incal-
culably altered. We are an essential part of time's stepping stone
to get to wherever it is going. Just as the millions of seeds and
humans before us combined to get us here, so we are here to
produce, influence, and affect the millions that will follow in our
small and very brief footsteps. Together, this seed and I are inextricably linked through the meandering course of time.

Bluebirds and Sky

T WO BLUEBIRDS (*Sialia mexicana*) quietly land on a strand of the barbed wire fencing next to me. They are both juveniles, proudly sporting their spotted breasts while they can, for as they mature the spots will fade into a solid coat of orange-red. One of them catches an earwig on the ground and thrashes it a few times before gulping it down. The other bluebird pants on the rusty fence wire. He is momentarily rejoined by the other juvenile who is soon back on the ground in the oak litter fluttering after another hapless earwig.[1]

A third juvenile joins the bluebirds and a titmouse whinnies from somewhere in the canopy above me while I watch another one gleaning something from a branch over my head. My eye is drawn back down to the ground where one of the bluebirds is foraging bottoms-up in the long blonde grasses which grew thickly in the spring beneath the shade of this tree. In a pale flash of blue, an adult female joins the youngsters. She's certainly not as blue as a male, but actually none of these birds have any blue coloring.

Like most birds with blue feathers, the blue is an illusion.[2] This appearance of blue color or pigment is called the Tyndall effect, and it is a common phenomena in stable, non-living tissues such as scales and feather. Remember that visible light is just a series of different-sized wavelengths from the sun. The long, slow wavelengths are reddish in color while the short, fast wavelengths comprise the upper end of the visible light and are seen as violet. All the other colors appear between these short and long waves. (Remember the acronym for the rainbow's colors? Roy G. Biv—red, orange, yellow, green, blue, indigo, violet.) The tiny little specks, motes, and grains that dance around in the air tend to absorb all the visible light colors except for the short, fast blue ones near the violet end of the spectrum. These blue wavelengths bounce around from particle to particle and reflect off of each other to create the blue of the sky.

The colors that we can see are the colors of light that are not being absorbed by an object and are being reflected back into the air. Grass is green because it absorbs all the wavelengths of light except the green waves; a shirt is red because it absorbs all wavelengths except red. White things reflect all the visible wavelengths while black objects absorb most wavelengths.

The same phenomena that makes the sky blue also makes bird feathers blue. Infinitesimal particulate matter trapped in the hollow, dead cells of the feathers reflect the incoming blue light. The feathers look blue, but if you crushed them they would turn dark gray. The hollow structures would be destroyed and all the light colors would be free to penetrate to the pigment surrounding the cell. This pigment is called melanin, and it absorbs all the light waves, thus making the feather dark. (It's also the pigment in people that produces freckles, a tan, or dark skin.)

Melanin is a true pigment, and like the rusty color on the bluebird's breast it is a chemical color as opposed to the blue, which is a structural color. If rusty feathers are put in a glass of water they will fade as the red-reflecting pigments dissolve. Blue feathers will stay blue until they start to rot and structurally break down.

The bluebirds draw me back once again to E.O Wilson. In poking through old ornithology books I find bluebirds consistently associated with goodness and kindness.[3] Dawson waxes rhapsodic that,

Bluebird is a gentleman, chivalrous and brave, as he is tender and loving. Mrs. Bluebird is a lady, gentle, confiding, and most appreciative. And as for the little Bluebirdses they are as well-behaved a lot of children as ever crowned an earthly affection.[4]

By the very nature of their interactions with humans bluebirds are "good" animals. They are insectivores and do not compete with humans for food but rather feed on many of the insects detrimental to our crops. They do not ruin buildings or structural supports to get to their prey. They nest near humans but not too close. They are handsome specimens and their voice does not intrude over our own. Dawson explains that the birds are from Mexico (*Sialia mexicana*) and since we won't let them speak Spanish they prefer to remain silent!

Appropriately enough, a young contemporary of Tyndall's named Maurice Maeterlinck wrote a play called *The Blue Bird*, about the folly of searching for happiness outside ourselves. He was a scientifically oriented fellow and I suppose he may have known about the Tyndall effect when he decided on a blue bird as the illusory symbol of happiness.

Particularly in eastern North America, bluebirds (as well as robins) are cheerfully greeted as the first prognosticators of spring. During World War II the refrain from one of the most popular songs of the war symbolically reassured that bluebirds would return to England at wars end. True bluebirds (those of the *Sialia* species) are found only in the New World. Bluebirds were probably never seen over British cliffs, but the songwriter used them to symbolize hope and happiness and lend optimism to the lyrics.

I hear the bluebirds gentle call and that song echoes in my head. It's a haunting reminder of air raids and black-outs, shattered buildings and bomb shelters. I think how lucky I am never to have lived through the terrors of a war. My American generation has never experienced a war like the ones our parents and grandparents lived through. We were even too young to clearly remember Vietnam. I realize how lucky we are to have had so much peace in our lives. Our wars are fought by missiles selectively seeking and destroying their targets from far behind enemy lines. My generation doesn't know about blood-spattered battlefields or homes in shards and splinters. We don't know about Wehrmacht bombs flying through the air instead of birds, nor do we know about yearning and hoping for peace in our own country.

As the morning sun slants over the hilltops, I whistle an imitation of the bluebirds soft, faint song, and I hope that we never will have to learn about such things.

Going Native

T HE BLUEBIRDS FLY OFF as Mick and I get up, shedding
brittle pieces of last year's oak leaves. We need
another little foray before the day gets even hotter, so
we cross the empty road and duck under the barbed
wire into a broad meadow of dried grasses and weeds.
The ground is perfectly yellow and crunchy under-
foot, and the hills are studded with dark clumps of oaks and
pines standing in the cool pools of their own shadows. The sky is
a happy blue and the sun is hot on my skin, searing me gold like
the summer grasses. Mick races ahead and chases shrieking
ground squirrels into their burrows. I follow at a more sensible
pace, toeing at scats, rocks, weeds, and am pleased when I see an
occasional bunch grass. These are perennial grasses native to
California. While their European cousins were pursuing their
own evolutionary tack in the fertile valleys of the Tigris and the
Euphrates, the California grasses, through their own evolutionary trials and errors, followed a divergent line of adaptation.

Taking a route diametrically opposed to their cousins, the
California natives developed deeper and well-established root
systems. Such a root system took time and energy to grow and
used resources which took away from above-ground production.
However, the deeper roots enabled the natives to take advantage
of groundwaters not accessible to their shallow-rooted cousins.

Once the root system was in place and able to provide an ample supply of water and nutrients throughout the long dry months, then bunch grasses spent their energies on seed production and growth. Because these perennials are long-lived, they could afford the conservative production of a few seeds at a time. If the weather was particularly bad in a given season, the parent plants might not have produced any seeds at all, but instead saved energy for their own growth and maintenance.[1]

Compare this evolutionary life-style to that of the Mediterranean grasses with their all-or-nothing evolutionary approach. As we have seen, the seeds of the non-natives are extremely opportunistic. Already adapted to the climate when they found themselves freed from their Spanish sailing ships, all they needed to complete their life's mission was a fertile patch of soil. The California grasses grew in well-spaced bunches, creating ample room between them for the new emigrants to establish themselves as they were carried from mission wheat fields into neighboring meadows.

The annuals were short-lived and did not need an intensive root system. When the ephemeral winter rains came, the dormant seeds of the annuals quickly sprouted and established a broad, fibrous root system. These short roots could soak up the available surface moisture, frequently preventing the moisture from percolating down to the roots of the perennial grasses. The annuals grew rapidly, put forth numerous seeds, and died. Extremely drought tolerant, the seeds endured until the rains came again the following winter.

Introduced livestock grazed heavily upon the sweet, abundant bunch grasses. Steadily the annuals sprouted between them and dropped their hungry seeds. Livestock continued to forage on the native grasses. Because they were not genetically programmed to handle such intensive predation the natives could not set seeds before their flowering tips were consumed.

Meanwhile the annuals made firm inroads into the native's habitat, reproducing and setting forth more seed while the bunch grasses remained unable to reproduce as quickly or suc-

cessfully. Grazing, tillage, and development increased and gradually the slow-growing perennials lost the evolutionary race to
the faster-growing annuals. The European grasses are more
common now than the natives, hence my pleasure at seeing the
bunch grasses.

I stop at an old salt lick next to a valley oak and look up into
the canopy. Acorn woodpeckers are quietly going about their
woodpecker business and this seems as good a spot as any to do
some bird-watching.

As I step into the shade of the oak tree I absently speak its
scientific name. It's odd to hear a voice, even my own, so for the
novelty of hearing them I repeat the words, "*Quercus lobata*." The
name means "fine tree with lobed leaves." *Quer-*, "fine," and *cuez*,
"tree," is the hybridized Latin and Celtic word for the oak
genus.[2] Because their leaves are characteristically rounded, the
valley oaks are defined by their second name, the Latin *lobata*.

There are 15 species of *Quercus* in California though only nine
are true trees.[3] All but three of them are found here on the central coast.[4] Like the perennial grasses their growth and reproduction is slow and unhurried.

There is an oak I sometimes stop at on my way into the
valley. It's a huge tree, and always alive with birdsong. I was sitting under it last spring, ostensibly reading research papers, but
really watching two Western kingbirds in a courtship dance. An
elderly man saw me and stopped to asked what I was doing. I
explained and he nodded, "It's a good tree." He said the tree had
been there since he was a little boy and that it was huge even
back then. Given the longevity of oak trees (they typically survive for 250 years) a Spanish soldier in Portolo's 1769 expedition up the Salinas Valley could well have passed by this tree in
its sapling stage.[5] With leaves for words and wind to give them
voice, I have often wished I could understand the stories the
oaks must be sharing with each other.

Along with the brown hills and idyllic weather, oaks complete the characteristic image of California. The exploring
Spaniards regularly recorded the abundance of lush pasturage

near clear streams and mighty oaks.[6] The landscape has changed since the conquistadors saw it, for today that huge valley oak fronts the now-dry Salinas river and the "lush pasturage" is someone's alfalfa field.

Changed too is Brewer's description of "more trees but less grass." The valley oaks he looked down upon were cut long ago to fuel a burgeoning charcoal industry.[7] Removal of the trees created more pasturage for livestock and increased crop fields. Continued grazing and farming over decades and then centuries prevented new oaks from establishing themselves, hence more grass and less trees. Ironically though, grasses and feed crops will sprout sooner, grow better, and stay greener longer in the comparably damper, cooler shelter of the oak trees than they will under the naked glare of the sun.

But agriculturists are only partially to blame for the lack of oaks. On a recent visit to my mother's house in Paso Robles we walked our dogs one evening through a nearby housing tract, "Shady Oaks," or "Comfort Oaks," or "Happy Oaks"—some such homey, good-feeling name—and I counted eighty-one houses to twelve oak trees. Around the undeveloped land surrounding the housing tract I found an average of two valley oaks per lot. Multiply that by eighty-one lots and it means roughly one hundred sixty-two oak trees were cleared to make way for the homes and driveways. I can only assume this tract was named in memoriam.

Just as ranchers and farmers can't take all the blame for oak decline, neither can developers. Although they profit mightily, the developers could not do so if they weren't filling a need. Over 31.5 million people live in California and we all need a place to call home.[8] As the population grows, we encroach farther and farther onto undeveloped land, until eventually we end up drastically altering if not destroying what originally attracted us.

The clear streams, themselves insufficient for our vast thirst, were long ago diverted. The unlimited grassy plains are now cultivated fields that require increasingly more resources, and the towering oaks that are synonymous with California are in danger of being felled forever. Admirable efforts are often made to preserve historic lone trees or groves but outside botanical circles little thought is given to the plight of these remaining oaks. Where they do remain the venerable trees are still under numerous environmental pressures, many of which can be traced back to our unwitting founders.

As noted, the non-native weeds and grasses are a robber-baron lot, staking out and claiming much of the available ground cover and its precious store of water. Like the native perennial grasses, oak seedlings are slow growers. As an acorn seedling sprouts it develops little rootlets that search the immediate soil surface for water. As it finds water its roots continue to grow, and given enough moisture and time the acorn will sprout into a sapling with a deep root system. A two-inch acorn sprout can have a tap root over two feet long. If no moisture is available upon sprouting, the acorn withers and fails to grow. A consequence of introducing the annual grasses to California was their spread into the oak woodlands. Their thirsty, shallow roots tend to usurp the available surface water from the acorn sprouts just as they do from the native grasses.

In addition to these below-ground pressures there are above-ground ones as well. Mule deer, which will readily browse the soft nutritious oak shoots, have traditionally been preyed upon by mountain lions. However, in the last two hundred years of their 45,000 year evolution mountain lions suddenly became popular prey for humans, either by outright killing or by the more insidious destruction of suitable mountain lion habitats.[9] With fewer mountain lions to control their numbers, deer populations in all but the most remote places remain unnaturally high, placing equally unnatural demands on the oak populations.[10]

Similar results occur with the eradication of the smaller carnivores from the oak habitats. With fewer foxes, badgers, bobcats, and coyotes, the rodent numbers swell and the nutrient-rich acorns rarely remain on the ground long enough to sprout.

When the acorns do manage to put out a few roots, hungry ground-dwellers such as pocket gophers and ground squirrels will not hesitate to make a meal of them. The odds against acorn seedling survival are tremendous.

I hear a soft tapping and find a white-breasted nuthatch crawling down the trunk head first. So many lives depend on these trees. They are the vegetative equivalent of rabbits. Like a rabbit, an oak will reproduce prodigiously. One tree can produce thousands of acorns and feed hundreds of organisms. If the habitat is suitable, some of the acorns will sprout and become mature trees. But *only* if the habitat is suitable. Before humans became such a dominant part of the landscape this reproductive strategy worked well for the oaks. They would produce thousands of seeds but only a handful would survive to adulthood. In a habitat with limited water and food resources this was ecologically necessary. But the landscape the oaks evolved in has changed. Whether they can evolve fast enough to survive in this altered habitat remains to be seen.

Nature moves slowly and methodically, correcting its problems as it goes. Humans often behave in just the opposite manner, moving quickly and erratically, ignoring problems rather than solving them. Human activities hundreds, even thousands of years ago can still cause very real problems today. The seeds planted two thousand years ago in a Mesopotamian delta still affect me. They affect the oak tree I'm leaning against, the veterinarian's income, Mick's health.

As a species human beings are very young: this is the stage in our development for learning and there is much to learn. The natural world, which has been here a lot longer than we have, is a great teacher us if we are wise enough to want to learn. Like E. O. Wilson's honeybee, humans have evolved through millions of years of contact with the landscape. We have come a long way with very many companions and as Wilson understatedly warns, "the destruction of the natural world in which the brain was assembled over millions of years is a risky step."[11]

Acorns

HE WOODPECKERS ARE QUIET, the nuthatch is gone, and all I can hear is a fly buzzing around Mick's head. We leave the relative coolness of the oak and walk back to the truck through the hammering heat. The sun is high enough that part of the truck rests in shade and I picnic on the tailgate, eating slices of Toscano salami wrapped around Provolone and melon. No one ever said roughing it had to be tough.

The abundance and variety of foods available to me reminds me again of my tremendous fortune. The band of Portola's soldiers I was day-dreaming about this morning were practically starving by the time they reached the Central Coast. There was game but it was hard to catch, and they knew little of the native flora. In their diaries, Costanso and Palou both tell how the local natives saved them with their offerings of pine nuts and acorn mush.

How did the people of this area—the Salinans, the Costanoans, the Yokuts, all the native American tribes of California—know how to prepare and eat acorns? [1] How they acquired this knowledge is as baffling to me as how the Greeks and Romans discovered olives, for both are vile in their unaltered states, bitter and unpalatable. Somewhere along the line somebody had to discover all the things I take for granted. I suppose if I asked a scientist or a historian how people learned what to eat, they would say they learned through centuries and centuries of trial and error.

If 150 years ago I had asked a member of the Salinan tribe how their people discovered that acorns were a life-sustaining food, they might have replied that Coyote or Eagle told them. One native California tribe had the following explanation.

At some point back almost beyond memory all the acorns were spirit maidens who lived in the sky. One day they were told that soon they would have to go to earth to be with the People who were being made. Naturally all the maidens wanted to look nice for their trip so they all started making hats. But before they had much of a chance to work on their millinery they were suddenly told that it was time to go to earth. The Black Oak Acorn had only completed a little of her hat so she simply put it over her head and that is why today the black oak acorns have small, insignificant cups. Tan Oak Acorn put on the hat she'd been making but it wasn't quite done.[2] That is why its cup is all frizzled and rough. Valley Oak Acorn and Canyon Oak Acorn were all ready to go with perfectly rounded and well-fitting hats, and as the Acorns tumbled to the ground they all closed their eyes and turned their heads up into their hats forever. But Tan Oak was jealous because her hat wasn't done, so she vowed to be the best-tasting acorn for mush, and it became so. The mush from the acorns of the Valley Oak and the Canyon Oak was black and not as sweet as that of the Tan Oak, and all the People knew it.[3]

So maybe that's how the native Californians realized the value of acorns. Or maybe the scientists are right. If so, imagine the vast number of unwitting martyrs who fell in the name of trial and error, but who eventually established reliable drugs and foods for successive generations: the unsung members of the Cro-Magnon Food and Drug Administration.

As they slowly migrated from Beringia down through the northwest and into California, the Asian people who would be known thousands of years later as the Salinans were no doubt doing much experimentation with the resources offered by their new environment. It is common for people to starve in new environments because they are not yet familiar with the flora and fauna. The new emigrants to Jamestown in the early 1600s were an appalling example. Of 600 original settlers, only 60 were still alive three years later and then only because the leader of their group, John Smith, had traded with the local natives for food.[4]

Like the tribes of the eastern United States, the western tribes also ironically fed the European explorers who would one day vanquish them.[5] By the time the Spaniards cruised up the Pacific coast of California the Salinans were well-adapted to their North American environment and able to offer Portola's malnourished explorers protein-rich pine nuts and acorn meal. The meal was a dietary staple for California tribes, with a Salinan family able to harvest enough acorns in one week to last them easily through the year.[6] Once collected, either by shaking the limbs or knocking them about with a long pole, the acorns were dried in the sun and stored in willow baskets lined with grasses or herbs which may have functioned as insect repellents. The women would then use the acorns as needed, cracking them open with rocks and grinding them into meal on smooth stone surfaces. These stones would be used for years. Eventually the continued grinding wore a depression in the rock which created a natural mortar to work the nuts in.

After the acorns were ground, the meal was placed in shallow pools in a creek or in baskets of water and left to soak until the water around it was clear. Only when the water ran clear was the meal fit to be eaten, for brown water around the soaking meal meant that bitter-tasting tannins were still being leached out. The meal was used to make a Cream of Wheat-like mush or soup, the "atole" which fed Portola's men. The meal could also be baked into biscuits or a sweet bread.[7] The bread dried up nicely and lasted for weeks, albeit it was black and hard.

John Muir, in his romps from glacial valleys to mountain tops, often took along nothing but a pocketful of acorn bread and Pliny the Elder wrote of it 2,300 years ago. He added the culinary tidbit that bread made from the acorn meal of female oaks was sweeter than that made from the male oaks. Pliny was a Roman naturalist, some of whose observations are more interesting than accurate. Oaks are monoecious ("one house") meaning that both male and female flowers are produced on the same tree. They are not dioecious plants, which produce either male or female flowers but not both on the same plant.

As nuts go, and it is a true nut, acorns on average are low in fat (10%) and high in carbohydrates (63%) with a 5% protein content.[8] The nuts are produced at varying times, depending on the species; a coast live oak will have mature acorns just six months after pollination while the acorns of the interior live oaks need up to two full years to mature.[9] The other oak species fall somewhere within this continuum of maturation. This staggered rate of reproduction was no doubt as critical for the human California natives as it was for the animal natives, allowing for consumption of at least one species of acorn throughout the year.

An average oak tree, depending on the species, will *conservatively* produce from 160—425 pounds of acorns during each reproductive period.[10] Multiply that by the conservative number of 1 tree per acre in an oak woodland and you have a ten-acre tract yielding 1,600 to 4,250 pounds of high quality food. Even if only half the oaks reproduce each year that is still a munificent food source. A family of six Salinan Indians would need roughly 2,100 pounds of acorns per year to feed themselves.[11]

Acorns fed the native people well, but they weren't the only ones dependent upon the bounty of the oaks.

Acorn Woodpeckers

AFTER LUNCH I RESUME LAZING under the live oak. Judging by the height of the sun it's only around eleven o'clock, but already the heat is intense and unbroken. It forces a stillness upon the landscape. There is not much that creatures can do in heat like this before their bodies reach dangerously high temperatures. This is the time of day when shade and shadow are eagerly sought. Lazing becomes not a luxury but a necessity.

From an oak grove faraway the dead calm is broken; something has spurred an acorn woodpecker to take up its distinctive, rhythmic noise-making, like someone sawing through green wood. Although the cartoon image of Woody Woodpecker was caricatured after a pileated woodpecker, his distinctive laugh was inspired from the acorn woodpeckers.[1]

Their official name, *Melanerpes formicivorus*, is both Greek and Latin. The Greek genus name is a blend of *melano* ("black") and *herpes* ("creeper") while the Latin species name combines *formica* ("ant") with *vorare* ("to devour").[2] Both names say a lot about this bird, although its common names are probably more accurate. The native Hispanics noticed its typical wood-boring behavior and dubbed it the *carpintero*, or "carpenter." Its English name more accurately reflects their dietary proclivities, as ants only make up a small percentage of the acorn woodpecker's diet.[3]

Although acorn woodpeckers feed heavily on acorns, in general woodpeckers are known to prey upon insects and larvae found within wood. To get to this food, woodpeckers often have to hammer into the wood, at a speed of roughly 650 centimeters per second.[4] Slamming my head against a tree at a speed fast enough to crumple car fenders does not seem like a lot of fun to me, but a woodpecker's head is adapted for that kind of impact. Compared to a human's, a woodpecker's brain is relatively small, thereby greatly reducing the amount of mass subjected to these tremendous pressures. Additionally, the brain is encased in a proportionately larger skull. Their skulls also have hollow, air-filled spaces inside rather than cerebrospinal fluid, like humans have. This lack of fluid eliminates the damaging "shock wave" effect of a hard blow. In the species that do a lot of wood-pecking, the force of the blow is delivered below the line of the brain case, and the frontal bones of the skull come down to tuck under behind the base of the bill. The bill itself is straight and sharp, and the tip is self-sharpening, which facilitates penetration. Furthermore, it is possible that muscle tissue around the skull assists to some degree in shock absorption.[5]

The woodpecker's tongue is uniquely developed too. As in humans, it is attached to a bone called the hyoid bone. With its attendant set of muscles this bone allows the tongue to be extended and retracted. In humans, the hyoid is wedged neatly under the tongue between the lower jaw and the epiglottis, but in woodpeckers this bone makes an almost complete loop around the skull, starting at the base of the tongue, extending around the back of the skull and ending in front above the nasal cavity. This adaptation enables the woodpecker to extend its tongue past its long bill and into cavities. Depending upon their feeding preferences woodpeckers have varyingly shaped tongues. Those that tend to spear prey have bristle-tipped tongues. Species like the acorn woodpeckers, who tend to collect sap and more easily accessible insects, have brushy-tipped tongues. All woodpeckers exude a sticky fluid at the tips of their tongues.

A: At rest or nearly so, retractor muscle (cross-hatched) of hyoid horns inserts well forwards.

B: When retractor muscle contracts and draws hyoid horns forwards, the loop of the tongue is raised and the tongue is shot far beyond bill.

C: When fully retracted, horns end at or in front of eyes, in cavity of upper mandible or (as here) even wound up around the eye.

Fig. 2. Tongue mechanism of a woodpecker. (From *Woodpeckers: An Identification Guide to the Woodpeckers of the World*. Copyright © 1995 by Hans Winkler, David A. Christie, and David Nurney. Reprinted by permission of Houghton Mifflin Company. All rights reserved.)

Acorns are the primary diet of the acorn woodpeckers, but they frequently catch flying insects and feed on sap. The first naturalists to report on the acorn woodpeckers assumed incorrectly that their primary diet consisted of grubs, like other woodpeckers.[6] They also surmised that acorns collected by these birds weren't eaten but were stored to allow the larvae inside them time to plump up. Numerous larvae inhabit acorns and oak trees and it would seem logical at first glance that these woodpeckers were excavating holes in order to find grubs rather than store acorns. Pliny noticed that the European woodpeckers found their prey by tapping around on the tree trunks searching for hollow spots in which to dig. He also offered another insight into Roman cuisine, writing that grubs were considered "delicacies to gourmands, and the large ones found in the robur [oak] are held in high esteem."[7]

When I'm splitting oak logs for firewood I see a lot of these fat grubs and wish I was gutsy enough to try one. Among people who have limited protein sources, grubs such as these are savory, highly prized treats.[8] Given my penchant for uncoagulated protein in the form of rare cow flesh, I wouldn't think eating a grub would be much challenge. But I am too much a product of my European roots: the eating of mammals and fowl has been sanctified for centuries, while the consumption of reptiles and insects is looked at askance. Such a culinary philosophy is only possible due to the wealthy abundance of warm-blooded game found in the countries of my Anglo-Saxon ancestors. So I scrape the fat white morsels into the wood scraps by the chopping block. Sooner or later the scrub jays will come around and eagerly gobble them up.

Pliny also advised that carrying a woodpecker's bill wards off bites from stinging insects and he considered woodpeckers useful for divination. According to the Christian bestiaries there was once a Roman king named Picus who used woodpeckers for just this reason. Pagan woodpecker legends also tell a tale of Picus.[9]

In his *Metamorphoses,* Ovid describes King Picus as a handsome fellow in love with a beautiful nymph. While out hunting in the woods one day, the goddess Circe happened upon Picus and immediately desired him. She conjured a phantom boar and sent it dashing into a thicket in front of Picus' horse. At the same time she created a dense cloud of fog which separated the young king from his companions. Having isolated him in the deep wood where he chased the ghostly boar, Circe threw herself at the handsome lad, but his heart was true. He steadfastly refused her advances. Repeatedly Circe tried to woo him and repeatedly he denied her. Enraged, she vowed revenge, and as Picus turned to flee he was astounded to see how quickly he was moving. Indeed his arms had been transformed into wings and he had become one of the many birds of the Roman woods. In addition, Circe cursed him with the knowledge that he would never again be with his true beloved and condemned him to continually beating his head against the trees in bitter frustration. Thus, the Latin name *Picadae* for the woodpecker family.

A Christian story about the woodpecker's origins has many of the same themes as Ovid's pagan tale. In the Christian account, Jesus came upon a woman in a red scarf baking bread outside her cottage. Being quite hungry Jesus asked the woman for some bread, whereupon she broke off a small piece of dough and started cooking it. In the pan the bread greatly increased its size and the woman said to Jesus, "This piece is too big for you. I'll make a smaller one." Two more times she pinched off a tiny piece of dough and cooked it up and two more times the bread swelled and she refused him the large portions. Angered by the woman's stinginess, Jesus turned her into a red-headed woodpecker. The bird flew away up the chimney and smudged itself all over with black soot.[10]

This story shows a curious blending of pagan and Christian mythologies. The central theme of both stories is about a deity who is denied, and out of vengeance creates the woodpeckers. In the old books I pore through, over and over I find one culture's mythologies borrowing freely from the mythologies of the cultures before them. With all this "borrowing" and overlap I find it amusing when cultures strongly purport their distinction and separateness from other cultures. I wonder how this can be when so many of them share the same origin stories, and indeed the same origins. How are war and genocide rationalized to keep identities separate when it is impossible to find the end of one identity and the beginning of another? When cultures are so closely intertwined separation is impossible.

Through the foxtail I am connected to Mesopotamia; through an acorn woodpecker to Roman pagans and third century Christians; through the acorns to the Salinans who once walked along this valley. Millennia pass and the blood of nations becomes mixed with the blood of people. The names and dates and heroes of mythologies mingle and blend like day into night. The distinctions become like dusk, not very light, but not dark yet either. The details of mythologies change but underlying themes connect the stories one to another. Chaos and darkness, then light and creation; falling from grace, then saviors and redemption.

When I find myself believing that I am separate from the world, I retreat to the valley and wrap myself in its balm; it is like having a second skin to put on when mine becomes too soft and raw. Coming into the valley is a feeling of coming home, it is a sense of being surrounded by my history. The sky above, the earth below, and all the creations in-between comfort me like a fuzzy old blanket. The valley's blanket is woven with the tensile threads of time and land, then dyed in a wash of living things and decorated with history. When I lose perspective and forget where I belong in the world I return to the landscape and wrap myself in its blanket. Then I remember, surprised I could have ever forgotten, that I am a part of everything and everything is a part of me. Our identities are inseparable.

Early Biology

THE SUN REACHES ITS ZENITH and begins its stately descent into afternoon but I am oblivious, lost in one of Sarton's many volumes of *The History of Science*. Considering the dryness of the subject these tomes are surprisingly readable, and no one illustrates better than Sarton the steps connecting ancient science to modern. Today's technological "miracles" are perched gingerly atop a massive pyramid of science. The insight, training, and technique that allow for scientific progress all stem from the foundation of science below them. At the bottom of this colossal pyramid are the Egyptians and Babylonians. From them the Western world garnered its knowledge of astronomy and mathematics. During the ensuing centuries Westerners would add greatly to the body of the pyramid.[1]

Although they had a pantheon of gods and goddesses upon which to blame cause and effect, the Greeks were the first people we know of to examine their surroundings with anything other than supernatural ("other than nature") curiosity. Explanations for natural phenomena were sought in true, logical reasoning rather than superstition and mythology. The Greeks were the first to realize that gods may have made roses but in so doing they created an object complete unto itself, fully capable of growing, reproducing and dying. This was a pattern suspiciously alike in all living beings.

Socrates was one of the early Greeks intrigued by these patterns. He believed in logic above all. Even if an argument led to a false conclusion, as long as it was soundly logical Socrates was happy. Plato studied under Socrates and developed this line of logical reasoning to an art form, and it was his student Aristotle who sought to link the logic of the mind with the facts of nature.

In the 4th century before Christ, schooling was only for the affluent. There were no schools as we know them today. Instead, men (very rarely women) would gather with an expert and discourse while sauntering about in togas. Aristotle's school in Athens was called the Peripatetic, a word still found in the dictionary 2,500 years later. It means "one who walks about." Scientifically not much happened after Aristotle. The Romans copied much of the existing Greek works, but they contributed little new knowledge to the young field. As far as science goes, the fall of the Roman Empire was not a loss; however, its collapse paved the way for Christianity. This powerful new religion would have dire ramifications for scientific endeavor.

According to the church fathers, to know God was to know nature; thus, one must study God in order to understand nature. Because God created all the natural laws He could change them just as well, so again, it was best to try and understand Him. Trying to find predictable causes for natural phenomena implied God was not responsible for that phenomena. Since God created all natural phenomena, such a course of study implied a disbelief in God. Denying the existence of God, or even the fallibility of God was heresy. To the rising young church heresy was an offense punishable by death. With this atmosphere greeting curious minds, it is clear why science languished for over 1,000 years.

Under constant scrutiny of the church all scientific investigations had to be undertaken with the aim of glorifying or exemplifying God's works. From this milieu came *The Physiologus* followed by the medieval *Bestiaries*, treatises intended to illustrate the Christian symbolism of plants and animals.[2,3] Lions were said to symbolize strength and courage, serpents the devil. Bees were industrious, cats lazy, and dogs faithful (hence the name "Fido," from the Latin for fidelity, or faith).

Some animals were given their associations for obvious reasons, for example the lion is strong, but I question its courage. I would be courageous too if I was the biggest carnivore in the forest, and of course dogs are faithful because they don't know how to use a can opener. Foxes were designated as cunning, though they are no more cunning than any other animal well-adapted to survival in its own habitat. A rabbit, a zebra or a cockroach may as well symbolize cunning. But this was the "science" of the day and it was taught for centuries.

When Plutarch wrote, "Where the lion's skin will not reach, you must patch it out with the fox's," he meant that when strength is not enough you must use cunning.[4] In 1532 Machiavelli made political use of this science when he claimed "The prince must be a lion, but he must also know how to play the fox," that is, a leader must be strong but must also know how to be sly.[5] When Shakespeare wanted to illustrate a crafty ploy he alluded to the fox, as did Aesop, Dante and Chaucer before him. One version of *The Physiologus* calls the fox "an entirely deceitful animal who plays tricks."[6]

Such a trick is to cover itself with red mud, lay on its back and puff itself up as if it were dead. When birds approach this supposedly dead animal to feed upon it, the fox jumps up and devours them!

The tree of science is deeply rooted in mythologies such as this. Is it any wonder then that the scientific name for the fox family is *Vulpes*, the same as the Latin word for cunning? But if foxes are so cunning, why is one of our native foxes hovering on the edge of an abyss that looks down into the black hole of extinction?

San Joaquin Kit Fox

P ART OF MY WORK as a biologist includes monitoring San Joaquin kit fox populations in north-central San Luis Obispo County. Though seldom seen, three species of fox converge in this area. Red foxes (*Vulpes vulpes*), although native to the eastern United States, were imported from Europe during the mid-17th Century to support the English passion for fox-hunting.[1] Since then they moved steadily westward and they continue to stretch their range in north-eastern California to the coastal edges. The gray fox (*Urocyon cinereoargenteus*) is a California native, as is the San Joaquin kit fox (*Vulpes macrotis mutica*). They are small animals, weighing less than my seven-pound cat (hence the name "kit" which means baby fox). Although the larger foxes are more abundant, ironically it is the smaller, less visible kit fox that gets most of the attention.

As often as they are seen by human beings, kit foxes may as well be called ghost foxes. Various factors contribute to their invisibility. Kit foxes aren't much larger than a tomcat and their overall buffy color camouflages them well against the tawny annual grasses. Like most terrestrial, predatory mammals in warm or temperate climates, kit foxes are nocturnal. They are not usually active during daylight hours when people are. Some predators can be stumbled upon during the day and flushed from their beds, but not kit foxes. They sleep well below ground in dens often converted from abandoned ground squirrel burrows.

Burrowing behavior, like a nocturnal lifestyle, is a common adaptation to warm climates. Where daytime temperatures are frequently recorded with three numbers, as in the arid kit fox ranges, it pays the resident animals to seek shelter below ground during the heat of the day. I have often put my hand into an old squirrel hole (checking to see if it is a possible kit fox den) and found them even on the hottest days of a Salinas Valley summer to be very cool, enviably so. The foxes surface at night when the thermometer may have easily plunged 50 degrees.

Originally these foxes were found only within the confines of the San Joaquin valley on the same gently sloping land that farmers and developers like.[2] As human settlement increased in the valley, its original occupants were forced to move on. Roughly 100,000 years ago both humans and foxes were busily evolving into the species they represent today.[3] A significant difference between the two species is that humans are marvelously adaptable and capable of surviving in any terrestrial environment. Sadly for the kit fox line, it evolved exclusively in the dry southwestern deserts and lacks the geographical flexibility that humans have. Yet despite the odds stacked against it this little species of fox is doing its damnedest to survive.

The kit fox is holding its own in the remaining areas of the San Joaquin valley that are not agriculturally developed, such as the large petroleum fields and the adjacent Carrizo Plains. Lack of prey, and the presence of gray fox in what could be a kit fox niche, made it unlikely that the kit fox could extend any farther west. But, remarkably, this little animal *has* moved farther west, right up to the foothills of the Santa Lucia mountains in Monterey and San Luis Obispo Counties. Although predators such as coyotes and badgers frequent their native ranges, here the kit foxes must also compete with neighboring oak woodland carnivores, such as bobcats, red foxes and gray foxes. Not only is the kit fox surviving the migration to a new locale, it is also surviving an increase in the number of animals that potentially prey upon it.

If the kit foxes in oak woodlands were limited to their traditional nocturnal diet of kangaroo rats, jack rabbits, and cotton tails, then the prediction that they would not have enough prey to feed on would be accurate. Remarkably though, the westernmost kit fox feed in large part on California ground squirrels.[4] Here is a nocturnal animal which has switched to a primarily diurnal ("active during the day") prey base.[5] This is a very distinct change in the behavior of an animal based upon its environment. In essence, it is evolution. The kit fox is changing and evolving in order to survive. This is Darwin's theory of natural selection in action, and I am an awed witness.

By switching from nocturnal to diurnal prey, the kit fox takes advantage of an extremely abundant food source, one not heavily utilized by its nocturnal competitors. Diurnal activity also decreases encounters with the larger carnivores that prey on the kit fox. A drawback, however, is increased exposure to diurnal predators such as golden eagles.

Pushed to the edge of the habitat that they evolved in, the kit foxes have had to quickly learn new tricks or perish. They are gamely struggling to survive: not just in a new habitat, but with increased predation, a major change in their food source, and human threats such as poisoning, shooting, development, and vehicular traffic. As the kit foxes crowd into the remaining habitats, the competition for suitable homes and adequate food begins to take its toll. The strongest, smartest and fastest of them will survive, taking the best of the available resources not already claimed. The rest will have to settle for leftovers or move into the edges of surrounding and differing environments. Here the stresses increase as the displaced foxes search for satisfactory shelter or edible prey. They may survive in these marginal areas but if their bodies are too strained from lack of rest, food, and shelter, then the female foxes will not come into estrus and they will fail to breed.

This is how with time, as much of the San Joaquin valley was converted from grasslands to developed lands, the San Joaquin kit fox population declined. This decline earned them a place on the Endangered Species List, which entails costly repercussions. According to federal law, all measures must be taken to protect these animals from extinction. This results in expensive development delays in habitat suitable for, or known to be occupied by kit foxes. It imposes strict regulations on how government facilities can use their lands. It restricts the type of poisons the agricultural community can use on their private lands. At a local vertebrate pesticide workshop (read: how to kill ground squirrels workshop) in 1994 the general consensus among many of the attendants was just to eradicate the whole damn kit fox population. One grain grower even stood and said "Let's just get this over with so that I can get back to killing squirrels and growing crops, 'stead of nursemaiding an animal that doesn't do us any good anyways."

To further that man's dilemma, ground squirrel populations thrive in agricultural areas where introduced grasses are raised. The soil is frequently turned over during planting, creating a loose, easily-dug texture that the squirrels favor, and the crops provide them with a perfect food source. Inadvertently, the farmer has done much to increase his squirrel population. Couple that with a decrease in natural predators, such as eagles, hawks, bobcats, foxes and snakes, and a virtual welcome mat is laid out for the California ground squirrel. The kit fox, which has had no direct role in this whole ecological drama, is suddenly and single-handedly responsible for the farmer's decreased profit margins.

Again, as with the oak trees, there is rarely one single factor that dramatically alters an organism's existence. Instead it is the debilitating onslaught of steady one-two punches that eventually brings a beast or a tree, just like a boxer, to its knees. When a referee stops the punches in time the boxer can eventually get up and recover; if the referee is too late the fighter may get hurt beyond the point where he is able to function. The Endangered

Species Act was designated as the referee. A referee's purpose is to prevent foul-play. They don't always make the right decisions, but the number of good calls usually outweigh the bad. The kit fox, despite being the underdog in this bout for survival, is fighting a fair battle. Its opponents are bigger, stronger, and far more cunning. If the referee makes a couple of calls in the kit foxes' favor, don't humans have enough of an advantage to concede them?

San Joaquin
Kit Fox

5052

I T APPEARS THAT KIT FOX NUMBERS in northern San
Luis Obispo are declining.[1] To determine these numbers our staff conducts various surveys throughout the
year. One survey method is to lay out a number of
lightly dusted scent stations. When animals come to
sniff at the lure in the middle of these dusty circles,
they leave paw prints. These prints (and other signs, such as scat,
tail-marks, and disturbances where an animal has rolled in the
dust) tell us what type of animals are in the area. Another
method involves driving designated routes at night while shining
large spotlights out each side of the vehicle. Both methods are
good for finding foxes, but they don't offer any data about individual animals. To get this data we trap the foxes. Every fall
baited live-traps are set out and captured foxes are marked with
numbered, metal eartags.

Capture success (the number of kit foxes caught) in the north
county has been very low in recent years, and handling opportu-
nities have been rare. A biologist is qualified to trap these endangered animals only after repeated, supervised practice with
handling them. Because so few animals were captured, it has
taken me years to accumulate the necessary handling time.

Last year's capture success after two weeks of trapping was
abysmally low. The few foxes we caught were already eartagged,

indicating no new animals were in the population. After an obligatory break for Christmas and the New Year holidays, we would finish our trapping session the first week in January. The two remaining trap lines historically yielded more fox captures than the completed lines, so I was confident there would be kit foxes to handle.

The first day of our last week found plenty of skunks and house cats in our traps, but no foxes. The same for the second day and the third. On the fourth there weren't even any house cats. On Friday morning, in the surreptitious gloom of first dawn, I drove by empty traps on my way to the office. Dejectedly gathering our handling equipment, my boss and I went out to pick up the traps in the growing light. Empty traps, empty traps, and skunks. Half-way through the route I was looking forward to an early lunch, but when we pulled up to trap number 42 there were the unmistakable ears of a kit fox silhouetted against the dawn.

Pleased that our last week wasn't a complete shut-out, I approached the trap. The fox was already tagged on the right ear, indicating she was a female (males are tagged on the left ear). I took the protective canvas tarp off the trap and wiggled my fingers over her head while I read the number on her eartag, 5052.

A typical kit fox is very docile, rarely doing more than hunkering down and making a small "mrph" noise in the back of its throat. 5052 was not typical. Barking and growling, she lunged against the cage and snapped at air. She was a feisty critter and I was looking forward to testing my handling skills with an aggressive fox.

I released 5052 into a special canvas handling bag and drew it shut, then hunched down on my knees to position the bag in the "V" made by my calves and thighs. Secured within these confines, the bag can then be carefully worked open, allowing the biologist to examine, tag, and gather samples from the animal. The fox was squirming in the bag and as I placed her in the angle between my legs I felt a small pinch on my thigh. I'd given 5052 just enough slack to nip right through the bag. There were no holes in my pant leg so I proceeded with the examination and forgot about the little snap. Within a few minutes 5052 was free. She darted a few steps away and shook herself then bounced off, head and tail held high. We finished the line and found nothing but more skunks.

Releasing skunks from live-traps is a smelly chore and when we returned to the office I had to change my clothes. It was only then that I realized I had two neat, small puncture wounds on my inner thigh. I scrubbed the blood away and poked a soapy toothbrush into the deep little bites. After ascertaining I still had plenty of rabies anti-bodies in my system (painless, pre-exposure rabies vaccinations are required for fox handling) I forgot about the bites.

Sitting here six months later under the live oak, I glance down at my thigh. Two tiny round scars stare back at me like little blind eyes. Number 5052 might lose her eartag some day, but she will always bear a scar where we tagged her. I will always bear a scar too, where she tagged me. And that suits me just fine.

Lightning

THE HEAT OF THE DAY is thickly upon us now. The branches of the live oak are low and touch the ground in places, enclosing Mick and I in a cocoon of shade. I lean my back against the edge of an old scar which smiles broadly across the base of the tree. It looks like someone tried to saw the tree with a chainsaw then abandoned the effort. I am hot, sweaty, grimy, and perversely contented. Even in the shelter of this grinning old tree the temperature is extreme; I guess it's around 112 degrees. It's hard to imagine now the cool, foggy rains that will come in the fall.

The central coast rains are often mild, what the Navajo call a "female" rain which falls softly and gently, allowing the soil to gradually absorb the water. Infrequent thunder storms result from the "male" rains, violent downpours produced by furious confrontations between cold and warm air masses. By fall and winter, air temperatures in this part of California are usually too cool to cause a reaction with the colder storms coming down from the north. As a result the central coast only averages five thunderstorms a year.[1]

My oak serves me well on a sunny day, but were I in one of those thunderstorms I might not be so inclined to seek shelter under it. In this grassy, rural part of the world oaks are the likeliest objects to attract lightning. Usually they are closer to the sky than anything else. Traveling around the county I occasionally see charred and jagged trunks where once healthy oak trees used to be; until they were visited by a 50,000 degree Fahrenheit bolt of lightning.[2]

Basically, lightning is just highly concentrated electricity. A bolt of lightning is really a number of smaller bolts that travel so quickly (in milliseconds) that to the human eye they look like one big bolt. The first bolt, or leader stroke, packs an enormous wallop of electricity, averaging from 20,000 to 30,000 amps.[3] (By contrast, the electrical wall outlets in our homes, which are potent enough, deliver only 15 to 20 amps of electricity.)

This huge concentration of electricity is built up in a thundercloud as a result of ice formation and turbulence within the cloud. As water droplets in the cloud freeze they are tossed high up in the cloud by internal updrafts. When the molecules of water freeze they tend to shatter, separating into lighter particles and heavier particles. The lighter particles have a positive charge and the heavier particles a negative charge. Continued turbulence within the cloud wafts the lighter positive pieces up to the top of the cloud while the heavier negative particles settle at the bottom of the cloud causing a distinct division between the positive and negative molecules. This separation creates a tremendous tension within the cloud which will eventually culminate in sparking.

As the thunderstorm advances over the earth, its bottom-heavy load of negative charges repel all the negative charges on the ground, like bullies on the beach pushing the skinny guys away from their girls. This leaves all the girls for the bullies, but in this case "the girls" are the positive charges. This creates a very strong pull between the ground and the cloud. We all know that opposites attract. (That expression originated with the recognition in the field of electricity that negative charges are attracted to positive charges and vice versa). These oppositely charged molecules want to be together but are kept apart by the distance between earth and cloud. When this tension builds to a critical level, sparks occur between the lower negative molecules and some of the positive ones floating highest above the earth.

Bear in mind that when this critical tension is reached, millions of sparks occur at the same time. All these sparks seek the path of least resistance to channel their energy into, and that is what our eyes generally perceive as the forks coming off a bolt of lightning. These forks actually precede the bolt, acting as a pathfinder by starting a channel for the bolt to reach to the ground. The bolt itself is created by the flow of all those negative charges in the cloud pouring along this pathway down to the positive charges hovering around the earth. This leader stroke forms the channel for the positive charges, which are drawn to the negative charges at the bottom of the cloud. This positive flow of charges is called the return streamer. One bolt of lightning usually has at least three of these exchanges although longer-lasting bolts, the ones we can see for a second or more, can have dozens.[4]

For centuries people have been observing an inordinate relationship between oak trees and lightning. The supreme powers of Zeus and Jupiter, arch-deities of the Greeks and Romans respectively, were symbolized by lightning and oak trees. The Norse god Thor was associated with lightning and oaks, as was the Lithuanian thunder god, Perkunas. The belief that oaks actually attract lightning is still so wide-spread in Europe that farmers often plant oak trees next to their houses to spare their structures from the fiery wrath of heaven.[5] In reality oaks get hit no more often than other trees, but they do seem to suffer the most obvious damages. While it is possible that the rough-barked trees have less resistance to lightning than smooth-barked trees, no one is certain exactly what mechanism causes extensive tree damage.[6] It was once thought that lightning took the path of least resistance, traveling easily over the smooth-barked trees and into the ground. Trees with rough bark slowed the easy flow of the lightning stroke. This increased resistance forced the lightning to seek a more conducive pathway, such as the sap within the tree. When the intense heat of the lightning contacted the sap, the sap instantly boiled. The resulting pressure in such a confined space literally blew the tree to smithereens.[7]

This "conductive pathway" theory has been generally discarded, although it does appear that rougher-barked trees like oaks and pines seem more affected by lightning than their smooth skinned relatives. In 1899 a survey was conducted on over 50,000 acres of forested German land and although oaks only made up 11% of the tree population, they accounted for

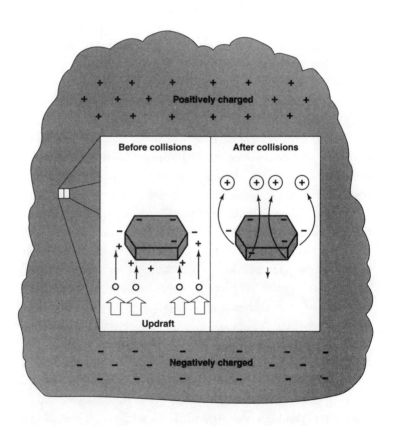

Fig. 3. Electrical charges in a cloud. (From *Severe and Unusual Weather.* Copyright © 1983 by Joe R. Eagleman. Reprinted by permission of Van Nostrand Reinhold.)

58% of the trees damaged by lightning. Conversely, beeches which comprised 70% of the forest only suffered 6% of the lightning-induced damages, making it look as if the oaks do indeed have an uncanny connection to the thunderbolts above.[8] While discussing oaks and their supposed affinity for lightning, Miss Carruthers in her 1879 book about flower lore, offered up the tantalizing tidbit that North American Indians thought themselves safe from lightning while sitting beneath a beech tree.

In this country lightning is the most lethal natural hazard, killing an average of 80 people annually.[9] The worst places to be in a storm are on hills or mountain tops, golf courses, under tall trees, or near wire fences. Tractors are dangerous too although inside a car is usually safe if metal is not directly touched. If it is impossible to get indoors the best option is to find cover in a valley, a ditch, or a grove of small trees away from larger trees.

Above all, don't seek refuge in a bell tower. During the Dark Ages churches were ordered to ring their bells during a thunderstorm. It was believed the pealing bells would drive off the lightning and the evil spirits accompanying it. This satisfied everyone but the poor bell ringers who were being electrocuted high up in the steeples. In 1786 the church mercifully reconsidered and rescinded the edict.[10] But still the pious weren't safe, for the invention of gunpowder soon followed. It had long been the practice to store weapons in church towers, and as no one yet understood the connection between high places, lightning, and gunpowder, it was common for entire churches to explode in a severe thunderstorm. Benjamin Franklin invented the lightning rod in 1756, but it was hard for people to abandon their beliefs. Many years would pass before people were finally convinced that lightning was a simple matter of physics rather than a direct manifestation of the wrath of God.

Western Fence Lizards

A PLANE DRONES, A FLY HUMS, the grass giggles under the firm tickle of the summer breeze...

I spy a coyote loping across the hill. It pauses and shakes its head in the thin shade of a shrub then continues running slowly along the slope. It finally disappears inside a deep gully that cuts the brown hill from north to south. Mick stands up to watch the coyote and I am surprised he sensed it from this distance. As the coyote disappears a cottontail above the wash runs the other way and a ground squirrel sends out its shrill, monotonous alarm, "plink! plink! plink!" It's as irritating as a water faucet dripping just as you are about to drop into sleep. The squirrel goes on and on and I gain a slight insight into why the locals like to sit against a tree in the afternoons, with a Bud and a .22, and blast away at them.

A young bluebird pokes at the ground three feet from where I sit and I count sixteen magpies flying up-field. At a distance they look like a school of silvery fish swimming against an aqua sky. Two more catch up then noisily they all take off followed by an even bigger group from a tree farther away. What prompts such mad activity in all this heat?

The squirrel ceases its warning and I am grateful. A cow ambles around a soft yellow breast of hill. Maybe the coyote spooked her and she suddenly realized she was a long way from company. Bluebirds forage boldly close to me, unfazed by my turning pages. Lizards drop off the tree trunk. The noise they make falling onto the crunchy dead grass is loud against the stillness. They sound like miniature Godzillas crashing through the Tokyo suburbs. Two of them chase each other round and about. Territorial dispute or romantic pursuit? Probably the former. It's mid-July and eligible females were mated by June, though males will defend their territories through the summer. I don't have a field guide with me, but these look like western fence lizards, which are pretty common to this area. Their Latin name slithers off the tongue, *Sceloporus occidentalis.*

In high school I hated the chaos of learning the Greek and Latin names for organisms. I couldn't fathom why I needed to learn this babble of dead languages. In hind sight I suppose it was for the same reason I had to learn Greek and Roman myths, historical names, dates, and places, the names of mountains, rivers, and countries I'd never been to, a foreign language, reams of literature and nightmarish mathematical equations. Not only our immediate cultures, but human culture in general is based on all this information. To not know this background is culturally tantamount to not knowing who my grandparents and great-grandparents are.

A specialized group of scientists, called taxonomists, are responsible for figuring out the relationships among organisms. They describe these relationships, and then categorize the organisms accordingly, in taxonomic sequences. Each grouping, or sequence, is called a taxon. The largest, most obvious taxon is called a kingdom, so all animals are put into the Animalia kingdom and all plants are put in the Plantae kingdom. (When this system was invented 200 years ago Latin was the predominant world language. In order to avoid confusion and create one common language within the scientific communities around the world, all taxons were given a Latin name.) From the kingdom taxon the classification becomes progressively more narrow and specific, going next to phylum, class, order, family, genus and species. In college I found the best way to remember this sequence was to remember the phrase, "King Philip Came Over For Good Sex." The first letter of each word in that sentence stands for the first letter of each taxon.

The fence lizards start off in the Animalia kingdom like humans do, and like us they have a nerve cord running from head to tail, so within the next taxon they are included in the Chordata phylum. From there they get placed into the Reptilia class, while humans are put into the Mammalia class. The next taxon is the order. Here we are classified with Primates and the lizards are found under Squamata, meaning "covered with scales." Within the taxons there can be subtaxons and this is where it gets *really* tricky. The generally accepted name for the lizard's suborder is Sauria, which is the Greek word for lizard.[1]

The family that all fence lizards belong to is Iguanidae. The taxons of genus and species further specify Western fence lizards as *Sceloporus occidentalis*.[2] (It was the custom when this system was established to italicize the genus and species names in order to clearly set them apart from the rest of the text in a body of work. For convention's sake, this formality still exists.)

In those dreaded high school science classes I never could have imagined I'd become a biologist. Now I am grateful for that taxonomic background. When I am on my hands and needs in a meadow trying to identify a flower, it's a lot easier to use my field guide when I have an idea of which family or at least which order to start looking under. And it's a skill I can use with any reference book, not just field guides. If I want to make a chocolate layer cake I look under the "Desserts" section of a cookbook. From there the desserts are often broken down into various categories such as cookies, puddings and cakes. The cake section may be further broken down into sheet cakes or layer cakes, and under the layer cakes I might find quite a number of varieties, including chocolate. But what type of chocolate layer cake, one with chocolate filling or raspberry-walnut? Unaware, we use taxonomic skills dozens of times every day.

Sauria is the lizard's sub-order, and its sister sub-order is the
Serpente. This is where snakes are categorized. The most immediate distinction between snakes and lizards is that lizards have
limbs. Like mammals they have a pectoral girdle to hold their
hind limbs, a structure lacking in the snakes. They can also
blink, unlike snakes which have no eyelids. Lizards have a fixed
jaw, not the hugely flexible lower jaw that the Serpente use to
engulf their prey. Lizards have blunt, rounded tongues, not long
and sinuous ones like snakes, which house their tongues in a
sheath within their mouths.[3]

Though certain morphological differences are obvious, these
two reptiles are still closely related on an evolutionary scale.
Despite this close relationship, lizards never seem to have engen-
dered the same animosity in humans that snakes have. The Funk
and Wagnalls Dictionary of Folklore even goes so far as to say,
"Everywhere that the lizard is indigenous (in all his genera,
species, and varieties) man has felt an inevitable affinity with
him."[4]

Lizards are mythologically associated with sunshine and
light.[5] In a 12th century bestiary it is noted that a lizard goes
blind as it ages, but then it "goes into a hole in the wall facing
east, stretches itself toward the rising sun, and its sight is
restored."[6] The association with sun may refer to a lizard's
regenerative ability. A fleeing lizard frequently loses its tail to
predators. The severed tail continues to wiggle, and often this
motion distracts the predator long enough for the lizard to
escape. But the lizard can grow a new tail.[7] The lizard's ability
to re-create a tail, as well as escape from death, is similar to
how the sun dies every night yet is reborn each morning.

Even though snakes and lizards are closely related, the latter
are far more similar to humans, engendering a greater affinity.
The most familiar thing about lizards is that they have four
limbs; they *look* more like us and they do not creep around like
snakes do. Somewhere in our past humans seemed to have developed a dislike for creeping things.[8]

Lizards as a whole tend to keep their tongues in their mouths and they discretely ingest their prey, rather than distending their jaws to slowly swallow a stunned quarry. They don't eat soft, fuzzy mammals either, but rather insects, so right away humans have more of an affinity with these "helpful" animals. Add to that their teeth, which are more like ours and not a mouthful of fangs—from asps to hypodermics to vampires, humans dread (yet have a morbid fascination of) long, sharp, needle-like objects. Furthermore, most lizards aren't poisonous so as a species we may have never developed a biological need to fear or dislike them. Unwitting pawns once again of our biophilias and biophobias.

As I sit here, a fence lizard is facing me. It leans insouciantly against a mat of bent stems. I can see its belly, as blue as bluebird feathers, hence their nickname "blue-bellies. The lizard cocks an eye in my direction. We stare. Abruptly it launches itself onto the tree trunk and races around to the other side.

No plane drones, no fly hums, no breeze tickles the grass… all I can hear is Mick panting next to me, a beautiful tawny dog the exact color of the dried grasses. His eyes and collar are milk-chocolate brown, as brown as the dirt at our feet. My faded jeans are the color of the sky, of the bluebird feathers, of the lizard's belly. I love how we blend in. The heat wraps a warm cozy blanket snugly around us and Mick's breathing is a steady drum beat…sometime later, I don't know how much later, I become aware of the sloping yellow hill that I am staring at. I can't remember truly looking at the hill or what my last thought was. I am only aware of emerging from a place within myself, vastly still and silent, that I didn't even know I had.

Datura

T HE DRAMA OF THE DAY is being played out as shadows begin their stretch across the stage of the valley. Mick and I need a stretch too and we saunter down the road in the opposite direction we went this morning. I hear a car coming long before I see it. A truck finally appears and it slows beside us. Jim Muller and Sons Drilling is painted on the passenger door.

"You alright?" the driver asks, a ruddy blond man, just past the age where he can eat and drink as much as he likes and never show it. Quickly, only vaguely aware that I'm doing it, I reason that if he has sons they are only around high school age but the truck is old and battered. I assume he is one of Jim Muller's sons.

I explain that I'm fine, just parked down the road and doing a little bird-watching. Prone as bird-watchers are to a reputation for eccentricities such as chasing birds in all manner of extreme climates, that answer usually satisfies everyone who stops to check on me.

He asks what I've been seeing and as I start listing the answer I see him lose interest. He politely lets me finish then says "Okay then, well good luck," and puts the truck in first. He and his partner, who is thin and dark, both wave and pull away. As I hear them drive on, I label the other man an apprentice. He looked

nothing like the blond man. Instinctively and almost uncon-
sciously I used my taxonomic skills to categorize these two men,
to put them in a place and perspective that makes sense to me.

Mick gets the "go on," his signal to resume wandering and I
stoop to examine a dark green plant sprouting on the roadside.
Its leaves are broad and flat, riddled with holes from hungry
insects, and its flowers are tightly closed into a long white tube.

Datura is its genus name, and common names include trum-
pet or moon flower, thorn apple, Jimson weed and Devil's apple.
The first three names are pretty obvious for the large white
flowers do look like trumpets when they are open, which is
often at night, and the datura fruit looks like a brown golf ball
with thorns. The latter two names were given to the plant by
soldiers going into Jamestown to quiet a rebellion. In their quest
to find edible food some of the soldiers tried a little datura. It
was not edible, and although no one died, their antics while
under the influence were enough to name the plant after the
town: Jimson weed, is a corruption of Jamestown weed. Around
the same time settlers discovered that datura fruit can cause
severe hallucinations, as well as death, so the plant was also
called Devil's apple.[1]

Occasionally I hear on the news that a couple of kids have
been hospitalized after experimenting with datura. It's a cheap
high but by all accounts not very pleasant. It is an extreme hallu-
cinogen as well as extremely toxic. Herbalist Michael Moore
warned that, "To dabble in Jimson Weed for dilettante pseudo
ritual purposes or to try to get stoned with it is a silly, gratu-
itous, and dangerous thing."[2] His recommendation, and mine,
would be to find a safer, more reliable drug to dabble with.

The active ingredients in datura are alkaloids, which can be
described as organic substances that tend to produce a distinct
reaction when ingested by animals. Alkaloids are found in a wide
variety of products such as coffee (caffeine), decongestants
(ephedrine), tobacco (nicotine), and tonic water (quinine), to
name a few. Datura has three primary alkaloids—atropine, hyoscyamine and scopolamine, the latter being the most common

of the three alkaloids. All three alkaloids are commercially extracted and employed as pharmaceuticals: atropine is an anti-spasmodic and was used to dilate pupils, hyoscyamine is likewise an anti-spasmodic, and like scopolamine is employed as a sedative.[3]

Because it contains so many antispasmodic agents, datura has been clinically used to relieve bronchial spasms associated with asthma. (Long before Western medicine arrived, indigenous New World people carefully smoked datura to ease asthma attacks.) Datura alkaloids also depress the activities of many of the organs under control of the autonomic nervous system, organs such as the heart and lung over which we have no conscious, direct control. In carefully limited quantities the alkaloids make useful sedatives.

Scopolamine is still used today in conjunction with morphine to produce what women at the turn of the century termed "the twilight sleep." They used this combination for pain-relief during childbirth but because it was so hazardous to the child its use was shortly discontinued. Today it is administered as a pre-anesthesia. The scopolamine depresses the cerebral cortex, enhancing the sedative qualities of the morphine, while at the same time lessening mucus and saliva secretions. On its own scopolamine is used to treat acute insomnia and delirium tremens.

For a number of years scopolamine was the primary constituent in motion-sickness pills and was grown commercially during World War II to ensure adequate supplies. For troops on combat carriers, scopolamine offered an 80% protection rate against sea-sickness. Among pilots it reduced a 7.5% air-sickness rate to 0.5%.[4] Imagine having to storm Iwo Jima after you've just finished a choppy and stressful ride in a landing craft. Or flying into enemy flak at the same time you're airsick. Without a doubt datura helped many vets finish their tours of duty alive.

Conversely, how many people died because of scopolamine and its sister alkaloids? All three of these solanaceaous alkaloids are highly toxic and doses must be administered in very small quantities. Though useful at the time, technology has replaced scopolamine as a motion-sickness preventative. Safer chemicals were discovered to do the job without some of the more unpleasant side-effects. In high doses these side-effects include extreme hallucinations. This was a quality valued among aboriginal New World healers who interpreted the visions as messages from their gods.[5] In the Old World, the herbalist Dioscorides prescribed one dram of datura root in wine for "pleasant fantasies." He cautioned however that two drams would "make one beside himself for three days" and that four drams was fatal.[6]

He also prescribed datura's relatives, henbane and mandrake: henbane as an analgesic and mandrake for those "upon whom being cut, or cauterized they wish to make a not-feeling pain." Dioscorides issued a disclaimer, for too much of the former "cause a mean disturbance of your sense" and the latter "drives out ye life."[7] Mandrake was to remain in use as an anesthetic up until the 16th century. Frequent references to the solanaceous plants throughout Shakespeare's works indicate that their usage was so wide-spread as to be known even to the layman.

Hallucination was a feature of the Solanaceaes purportedly used by witches of the Dark and Middle Ages to commune with their Devil, thus the notorious reputation of plants such as belladonna, henbane, datura and mandrake.[8] During this period of history medicine and religion got horribly bollixed up, and as a result thousands of people died cruelly and needlessly.

Christianity triumphed over paganism during the 4th century BC, and in order to avoid persecution many practitioners of the old faith seemingly adopted the new religion. These people lived in villages and small towns distant from larger cities swayed by Christian seats of power. Away from this constricting influence the country people continued their traditional beliefs and practices.[9] This was the beginning of the exclusion of science, and as medical innovation is closely allied to science, the Christian dogma was in effect the death knell for medical growth as well.

Just as there was no need to investigate nature's workings, so there was no need to seek cures for disease.[10] There were only two possible etiologies for disease: mental illnesses were clearly an indication of demonic possession, and physical afflictions were caused by God. If God afflicted a person He did so for a reason. Disease was a direct sign of His displeasure. The Christian god was infallibly just, therefore the afflicted must have done something wrong. Disease became a trial to be borne, much as in the manner of Job. To ameliorate or lessen the effects of the disease through the intervention of medicines was to lessen one's faith and hence one's belief in God. This would only serve to further incur His wrath. All that could be done was to pray and repent. Cold comfort indeed, although the monks in the monasteries did dispense medicines for minor ailments. This served the dual purpose of creating a need for the Church among the newly converted pagans, as well as increasing the local popularity of the monks.

Generations passed while the Church broadened its reach. Many of the pagans incorporated, then gradually adopted Christianity. Power and authority drained from the community and increased among the Church and state. Schisms between good and bad, nature and spirit, Christian and pagan, became larger, unbreachable. Experimentation with herbal efficacies was looked on with increasing suspicion. Those that continued to practice the old ways were frequently punished by a ghastly death, but those that retained this ancient knowledge at least had some sense of power.

Although the Greeks were not entirely rational when it came to many of their medical treatments, through the works of men like Dioscorides steps were being taken to find organic rather than superstitious causes and cures for illness. As Christianity ascended, the printed secrets of the pagan healing arts were kept cloistered in rare manuscripts and codices throughout Europe. Asia, which still had an active interest and ability to pursue secular knowledge, was also a repository for these documents. There was an additional hiding place for this illicit knowledge. It was in the memory and legacy of the pagans. Where the local monastery could not or would not aid in the treatment of physically ill individuals, it was only natural for the villagers to turn to someone who remembered the old treatments. Women have traditionally been care-givers and healers, passing their knowledge down from grandmother to mother to daughter over many decades. The women of the early Dark Ages were no exception and for some of them this would prove fatal.

Man has inherently sought explanations for misfortune and inequity and the Christians were no exception. They readily found the Devil to be a handy scapegoat.[11] And just as God needed angels to serve him on earth so did the Devil need helpers. Thus the origins of the witches.[12] Because they were supposedly so much easier to tempt than men, women were frequently accused of being witches. Especially suspect of satanic collaboration were women who still possessed knowledge of the pagan ways. Such knowledge included the use of herbs for various and sundry purposes. Admittedly there were women who professed to be the Devil's helpers, either through coercion, out of sheer stupidity, or to have the upper hand in a man's world.

Accused witches were more likely motivated by economic gain rather than satanic religious purposes, for poisoning of rivals, both romantic and political, was not uncommon in the Middle Ages.[13] The women who had clung to the old healing arts knew which herbs were potentially fatal and could command a fair price for them. Among the more powerful poisons in the so-called witches arsenals were the Solanaceaes, henbane and mandrake, belladonna and datura.

When I look at a datura plant I see continuity, a legacy of information spanning continents, decades, institutions, and political climates. In the introduction to his wonderful herbal le Strange marvels:

> Another point that constantly impresses me is that over the centuries every single plant mentioned in the following text, whether poisonous or not, has been sampled for food, or patiently experimented with in an effort to find out about its medicinal use. How many people succumbed to

the more virulent sorts before the proper dose was found will never be known—but it was surely many thousands. Nevertheless, these simple cures have continuously and slowly evolved over the centuries from nearly every country in the world.[14]

When I look at a datura plant I see knowledge, wisdom that has endured and survived trial and error, use and misuse, for century upon century. The gifts of anesthesia are known to us today because of what has been passed along to us. We have greatly modified many of these drugs, but it was men like Dioscorides, and women who were burned at the stake, who built upon the works of the others before them, and whose works were in turn used and added to by their successors. I enjoy almost immediate relief from a headache because somewhere far back in time someone made it known that a tea from the bark of willows can ease head pain. Later on someone identified that ingredient in willow bark as salicylic acid. Someone else learned how to extract it, and someone else formed it into a little tiny pill. All I have to do is put the pill into my mouth and swallow.

When I look at a datura plant I see heroes, men and women who enabled my easy life. So many other people have done the hard work for me. Women practicing their craft of curing through plant-lore were burned alive for their beliefs, yet others picked up where they left off and their knowledge survived. Over 400 years ago, the Christian church condemned Michael Servetus to be burned alive.[15] Servetus, a Spanish physician, refused to recant his theory that blood flowed from one side of the heart to the other via the lungs. We now know that it does, but at that time such a notion was contrary to the official Church position on medical matters. Galen, a Greek physician in the 2nd century AD, was *still* the reigning medical "expert" of the Church and any medical work which contradicted him was construed as heresy. Servetus died and his works were burned, but his heretical notions planted a seed in the minds of other men. These seeds would take root and flower in the more optimal time to come.

Look at a datura plant. Like me, like William Blake, maybe you too can

> ...see a World in a Grain of Sand
> And a Heaven in a Wild Flower,
> Hold Infinity in the palm of your hand
> And Eternity in an hour.[16]

Band-Tailed Pigeons

A LITTLE FARTHER DOWN THE ROAD we enter a bend and flush about a dozen band-tailed pigeons (*Columba fasciata*). They are beautiful birds, though easy enough at a glance to confuse with the far more common domestic pigeon (*Columba livia*). According to experts, there is little distinction between pigeons and doves.[1] Both are plump-bodied, small-headed and stubby-legged. They share similar habits, such as bobbing their heads when they walk, a seed diet, a cooing song, and both their males and females produce crop milk for their young. (Crop milk is a fatty, protein-rich substance from sloughed crop tissue.)

I watch them fly away and I ponder their similarities to acorn woodpeckers. My scientist knows they both depend upon oak woodlands for food and shelter. My poet knows they both have a rich pagan lore which was later incorporated into Christian lore.

Worship of these birds goes as far back as 5,000-2,000 BC.[2] The Sumerian goddess Astarte had a shrine at Hierapolis which was decorated with doves. One of these decorative doves could even be removed from the building. Every year it was taken to the Mediterranean Ocean to bring water back to the shrine in order to commemorate the saving of Deucalion's ark during the Deluge.[3] Deucalion was the pagan version of Noah. When men on earth were being wicked, Zeus sent a great flood to destroy them. Of all these men he chose to spare only Deucalion, and his wife Pyrrha, who were to become the progenitors of the human race.

The Christian version of this story substitutes Noah for Deucalion, but in both myths the men and their wives find refuge on a mountain top and repopulate the world. It's not clear exactly what role the dove had in Deucalion's trials, but in the Christian account the dove was released from the Ark and returned with an olive branch, indicating the waters had receded and the flood was over. These stories are so similar one could assume a dove served the same purpose for Deucalion.

For the pagans the dove was associated with Astarte, Aphrodite, and Venus, all goddesses of love. This tradition continued with the Christian church where the dove is highly symbolic of the Son of God, the Christian personification of love. The Columbidae (the bird family that includes pigeons and doves) are traditionally symbolized in Western culture as paragons of peace and gentleness. By and large these are relatively docile birds, though in captivity there can be bloody altercations.[4]

Like all their relatives the band-tailed pigeons are social birds. They feed and roost in flocks, and during their annual north-south migrations, individual flocks often travel together to create one huge flock.[5] These pigeons are slow breeders, laying only one egg per clutch. The number of clutches they lay depends on the length of the summers and availability of food where they nest. In their northern ranges they usually only clutch once, though in the southern latitudes they may nest two or three times a year. In a world without hungry human beings, this slow rate of reproduction was probably critical to the survival of a bird with long life spans and limited food supplies.[6]

Pigeons have weak bills, no talons, and fat, tasty bodies. Their primary defense against predation lies in the great speed, strength, and agility of their flight. The former qualities make it an attractive lure for the novice game hunter while the latter make it a particularly challenging quarry for the expert. When the birds are migrating in huge numbers they become far easier targets for someone with a shotgun, hence local concentrations can be severely decimated by only a few hunters.

This happened in the eastern United States with the passenger pigeons (*Ectopistes migratorius*). In a little over 300 years these birds were hunted into extinction.[7] In 1911, with only a handful of captive passenger pigeons extant, there was a great slaughter of migrating band-tailed pigeons on the western coast of the country. The appalling take prompted an immediate public outcry. This led to federal legislation which eliminated all band-tailed pigeon hunting for the next 18 years. Since then, carefully controlled bag limits have helped to keep their numbers steady.[8]

Mick and I return gratefully to our tree. He laps water from his dish and I guzzle from a cold, wet bottle of iced tea. We will soon sweat out the liquid and need more, it's a physiological cycle. Everything is cycles.

The pigeons migrate, creating an annual cycle. They winter as far south as Central America and summer as far north as Washington state. Individual birds have cycles as well, from birth to death. I wonder if Martha, the last surviving passenger pigeon, was ever lonely in captivity. I would think a flocking bird would have a sense of unease in isolation. Populations cycle, from creation to extinction. Was the last passenger pigeon in the wild a male, and if so how long did he coo tremulously for a female? Or was the last wild bird a female? Did she band with another species or fly restlessly in search of other band-tailed pigeons?

The stories of these animals cycle as well, from one culture to another in barely veiled guise. Ecclesiastes wrote of the cycles of time.[9] He offered that there was no new thing under the sun. He knew that nothing changes, that everything has its season, and every season passes, then returns. I find comfort in these cycles, in knowing that very little truly changes.

Passenger pigeons weren't the first animals to become extinct. They won't be the last. Before there were *Homo sapiens* there were other species of humans. Over one and a half million years ago *Homo erectus* and *Homo habilis* may have shared the same habitat. Their species winked out like dying coals against a black night. But then a new species of man, the Neanderthal, walked the land for almost 175,000 years. Eventually, they too faded into a dim corner of history's memory. Ours is the only surviving *Homo* species, and already we have been around for 100,000 years. Who or what, if anything, will we become next?

Oak Galls and Gall Wasps

NDETERRED BY THE INTENSE HEAT, blue birds forage in
the road. A hot dry wind blows down the valley, bend-
ing the withered yellow grasses before it as it comes. I
see the wind before I hear or feel it. It kicks up a dust
devil and hurls a grass stalk on a lone jerking dance
over the road, its tan head bobbing macabrely on its
thin body. The wind continues on, kicking up the debris in front
of it like a little boy walking aimlessly down a sidewalk. A cooler
breeze from the west suddenly confronts the rush of dry air
cruising down from the north, but it's July in the valley and the
moist ocean breeze quickly withdraws in the face of superior
firepower.

The hot rush of air almost blows away what is resting in my
palm. I picked it up on our walk and it looks like a small apple
carved from wood, but it weighs about as much as a paper
towel. There is a tidy hole about a quarter of an inch in diameter
drilled into the ball and three smaller but equally neat holes
about the size of pinheads. A sort of black soot covers the
weightless sphere.

As often happens, curiosity overcomes my impulse to leave
nature alone and I pry the ball open at one of its sutured seams.
Clearly it was a living thing at one point. Inside the wooden skin
I find a golden brown network of spongy tissue with the texture

of a malted milk ball. A few rounded chambers toward the center of the ball are sprinkled with what look like pepper grains. I wish I had a microscope on me but I guess that the specks are either desiccated wasp larvae or feces, for what I have broken into like a thief is an oak gall.

Galls are common organisms on oak trees. One valley oak can have thousands of galls on it and not all of the same type.[1] Some are star shaped and pink, some look like dunce caps, and some grow along the stem like a corndog. The gall I'm holding is often called an apple gall. The young galls are shiny apple-green and covered with a waxed-satin skin very much like an apple.

Gall is another word for bile, a bitter, yellow acid produced by the liver to help the small intestine break down fat. Because of its bitterness and acidity "gall" has come to represent something particularly rancorous or irritating. A gall on an oak tree is the result of an irritant; approximately 2,000 types of organisms can stimulate a plant into production of one of these structures or galls.[2] A specific organism will direct the plant to produce a specific type of gall, and gall experts ("cecidologists") can look at one of the myriad forms of a gall and tell which organism made it.

California gall wasps (*Andricus californicus*) make apple galls.[3] These wasps from the Cynipid family are harmless to humans and not much bigger than the body of the letter i. Cynipid wasps are a biological oddity in that they don't follow the normal boy-meets-girl code of reproduction: in a number of cynipid species the females can reproduce without fertilization by males.[4] This may seem odd, but when environmental stresses cause the death of a large number of the young wasps produced in a year, then it makes good evolutionary sense for the surviving females to reproduce themselves. Their chances of successfully bearing young from asexual reproduction are far better than their chances of successfully bearing young through the trials of sexual reproduction. The females can produce more young on their own and thus better the odds of short-term survival for the species.

The long-term drawback of such a mode of reproduction is that only the female passes on her genes. There is no fresh genetic input from differing males. This reduces the genetic variability of the young wasps, leaving them with less genetic flexibility to adapt to varying environmental circumstances. Such a disadvantage is probably one of the reasons this type of reproduction, called parthenogenesis, is not more common.[5]

Gall development can be initiated either chemically or physically.[6] In the former manner the wasp will inject her eggs into the softer tissues of an oak (such as leaves, buds or roots) and the nucleic acids (the DNA) of the egg mass react with the oak's cells. This produces a very species-specific plant tissue growth that encapsulates and isolates the wasp eggs. Physical stimulation, as occurs with apple galls, is precipitated once the eggs hatch into larvae and begin chewing on the plant. As the larvae chew they produce an enzyme (a catalyst that initiates biological reactions) which like the nucleic acids "tells" the oak cells what type of gall to make. Again this stimulus causes the oak to produce specialized tissues to cover up and isolate the irritant from the rest of the tree.

Ironically such encapsulation protects the developing larvae by locking them up in a well-stocked larder where they leisurely pupate and eventually emerge as adult wasps. In trying to defend themselves, the oaks perpetuate their own demons. However, upon closer inspection of the large hole in my apple gall it would appear that these larders are far from impenetrable. The hole was probably made by a bird in search of the fat, juicy, protein-rich inhabitants pupating within, and other animals benefit as well.

As the larvae chew away at the oak, they convert its cellulose into a type of sticky, syrupy sugar. This "honeydew" attracts bees and ants which in turn feed insectivorous birds like flycatchers, bluebirds and kingbirds. The wasps and galls also support a host of minute creatures which will invade the larval sanctuary of the gall, attacking not only the resident larvae but consuming their home as well. Most of these tiny assailants are midges, wasps, weevils, mites, and moths. Those that actually feed on the gall itself are called inquilines, from the Latin *inquinus* or tenant. Once the gall falls from the tree it will likely be eaten by squirrels or mice who seem unfazed by the high concentration of bitter tannins.

Tannic acid is another in the oak's arsenal of defenses against predation, but as quickly as one organism can create a defensive strategy another will evolve a way to get around it. Animals like mule deer and ground squirrels, which feed regularly on oak products, produce a specialized salivary protein that binds with tannin chemicals.[7] Without this protein, tannins will bind in the digestive tract to enzymes which initiate protein breakdown. With these enzymes "caught" by the tannins they are unable to initiate digestion of the proteins in the acorn or oak leaves. The animal with no tannin defenses is in effect starving itself by eating food its body can't use. Although a mule deer can excrete around 98% of the tannins it ingests, it still has to balance the rate at which it can process the tannins against the rate it consumes them. It is a ratio much like the alcohol intake chart the Department of Motor Vehicles issues—depending on body weight and time between drinks it shows how much alcohol one can drink and still remain sober.

Thinking of the chart reminds me that I have a beer nestled in the cooler under a layer of melting ice. I get up from under the oak but Mick interrupts my move toward the cooler to begin his nightly re-enactment of the dinner dance. First he prances coyly, waving his brushy tail and swinging his hips against my legs. If that doesn't work and I am within range, he starts gently pawing at me, and staring at me with shining brown eyes. If that fails he'll stare at me and woof softly until I either feed him or tell him to knock it off. If I tell him to quit, he'll flop heavily to the ground and put his head on his paws to watch me carefully and not without reproach. Should I make the slightest move toward him the dinner dance starts all over again.

Rather than go through the whole scenario tonight, I momentarily forego the beer and prepare his dinner. As I swing toward him with dish in hand, in the last ecstatic moment of anticipation he dances on his hind legs like a crazed circus bear. These are the closing steps of the dinner dance and what Mick lacks in style he more than compensates for with enthusiasm.

Mick is a simple companion. His wants are few and easily provided. His joy over dinner, in chasing squirrels, over being petted, is a continual source of wonder for me. Mick reminds me every time I look at him that the best things in life are very simple. Like breaking into an oak gall and discovering whole worlds of life. It's like uncovering a chest full of buried treasure right under my house. Each gall, small and unassuming as they are, is a nugget of gold for so many.

I pull the beer from the cooler. My chest is full of an elemental reverence. It is a vibrant, almost painful awareness of just how sweet, how enduring, life is. I twist the cap off and tilt the wet bottle toward my lips. But then I pause. I pour the first sip out onto the ground. The oak leaves whisper softly and then I drink.

California Ground Squirrels

T HE SUN IS SINKING behind the hill to the north and is blocked by a tall line of pines and blue oaks on the ridge top. At last it's comfortable enough to leave the haven of the live oak so I pull a folding chair from the pick-up and sit near the tailgate. My face is crusty with salt and I lick some off with my fingertips; it complements the beer. It is silent, still too hot for the birds to start their evening foraging, but I gaze through my binoculars anyway. I sweep them over a valley oak across the field. Softball-size holes surround its base.

Were I in Scandinavia I might be captivated by the story of the grandmothers: that the fairies live amongst the roots of the oak trees and that these holes are the entrances and exits of the "wee people." [1] But I am not in Scandinavia and I know that these holes are the entrances and exits of the oak grassland's most ubiquitous inhabitant: the California ground squirrel. *Spermophilus beecheyi* is its scientific name, *spermo* and *philus* respectively signifying "seed" and "lover." [2] The species is named for Captain Beechey, a British navigator from the early 1800s who stopped in California while on his way up the Pacific coast to the Bering Straits. [3]

The captain thought the squirrels "rather a pretty little animal," though I don't know how many people would agree with him. Ground squirrels aren't terribly popular with most Californians, although indigenous peoples relied on the ground squirrel as a dependable food source.[4] Today they are regarded more as a nuisance. They undermine buildings, roadways and trees. They carry infectious disease. They scrounge orchard fruits and field crops. They compete with livestock for forage. Their list of mischiefs is long.

The earliest and most frequent complaints about ground squirrels began with the well-developed missions found up and down the state.[5] Recall that ground squirrels are particularly fond of developed lands where they find plenty of weed seeds and easily dug soils. This is exactly what the Spanish fathers provided all around their missions. The ground squirrels also favored the fields where livestock grazed. The trimmed grasses provided excellent views from their burrows, unlike the longer, predator-hiding grasses of the ungrazed areas. The war against the rapacious ground squirrels had just begun.

By the mid-1800s squirrels were frequently referred to as serious agricultural pests and in 1869 California passed a bounty on squirrel tails. This was ineffective at best and in 1874 it became state law that all property owners had to kill whatever squirrels they found on their land. This abatement policy lasted sixteen years until it was deemed unconstitutional and struck down. The offer of free poisoned bait was the only official abatement policy until bubonic plague broke out among ground squirrel populations in 1909. At that time, the United States Public Health Service took control of their eradication. After an initial decline in squirrel numbers (due to their deaths from plague), the plague-resistant members of the population quickly rebounded. Once again there followed a vigorous campaign to decimate their numbers. During this period an estimated 22,000,000 squirrels were killed in California, at which time they were thought to be under control.[6]

With the outbreak of World War I, the squirrels were again prime agricultural nuisances. Food was strictly rationed in order to provide plenty for personnel fighting overseas. Grain and seed crops had to be protected from hungry ground squirrels. Control policies shifted to the County Horticultural Commissioners, the federal Biological survey, and local farm bureaus. All of these agencies mounted intensive educational campaigns aimed at the complete extermination of the ground squirrel. The abatement law of 1874 was again enacted and (in an ever-popular public relations move) even school children were targeted, with cash prizes no less, in the hopes that they would bring their parents into the slaughterous fold. Tons of poisoned baits were provided at very low cost. The authorizing agencies also offered as much expertise and assistance possible. All this in an effort to make the mandatory eradication seem more voluntary, "to instill a desire in the mind of the ranchers to eradicate the squirrel and gopher pests."[7]

A year later the County Horticulture Commission became the Department of Agriculture, but their mission remained the same. Over the next decade they would distribute 10,000 *tons* of poison enabling them to kill 75 percent of California's ground squirrels.[8] Mandatory abatement was rescinded in 1933 although authorities retained abatement rights on properties where squirrels were deemed troublesome. It was still the Department of Agriculture's job "to instill a desire in the mind of the ranchers" to eliminate the ground squirrel. The Public Health Service did realize though that the best way to fight the plague was not at all; natural deaths from the plague would automatically check ground squirrel numbers.

For decades California agriculturists were programmed to vilify the ground squirrel. The 1960s heralded a growing public awareness of biological concerns, including long-term effects of poisoning on ecosystems. Slowly the public began to call for changes in eradication policies, but by this time, agriculturists were trained to eliminate ground squirrels on their property using poisons. They were not necessarily interested in slower-acting, long term biological controls which did not show immediate results. For roughly the last hundred years California mythology taught that squirrels were evil little beasts stealing food from the mouths of sons dying for their country. When they were not busy doing that they were spreading pestilence and plague. A healthy biophobia has been evolving around the California ground squirrel. That is unfortunate because this animal plays a vital role in the ecology of oak savanna communities.

As their Latin name suggests, California ground squirrels are granivorous, or grain-eating. Seeds are their preferred food source. At certain times of the year when seeds are hard to find they will switch to other foods.[9] In the late winter and early spring they eat green herbage, just as cattle do. Then they compete with livestock for the same food source. That's the bad news. The good news is that many of the squirrels are still hibernating at this time. Most of the squirrels foraging above ground in the coldest, wettest part of the year are last year's young. They didn't store up enough fat over the summer or develop enough of a seed cache in their burrows so they cannot hibernate through the winter.

As the rainy season wanes, adult females are next to emerge from hibernation for soon the demands of pregnancy will be upon them. Adult males can usually afford to emerge later in the spring. An adult ground squirrel needs a daily average of 61,170 calories. Green forage yields roughly 4,650 calories per gram. Because a squirrel is better adapted to seed digestion, it only digests 49% of the green forage it eats.[10] An adult, non-lactating ground squirrel needs to eat about 33 grams of green forage per day. On a seed diet however, a squirrel is able to use 87% of the food it ingests. And because a seed diet provides an average of 5,006 calories per gram, the number of grams required daily drops to around 17. It is in the squirrels best interest to switch from forage to seed as quickly as possible. In late spring and summer, when the seeds become available, they do just that. In urbanized areas and around crop fields many of these seeds are from weed species, thus ground squirrels limit the spread of aesthetically or agriculturally undesirable plants.

During this time of year a squirrel will spend about 7 hours a day above ground.[11] Of this time only 50% of it is spent in foraging; the rest seems to be dedicated to basking in the sun. "Shadow-tail" is the literal Greek interpretation of the word *sciuros,* where the word squirrel comes from. It was a popular early belief that squirrels used their tails to shade themselves from the sun.[12] Popular modern belief suggests that basking in a warm sun might benefit the squirrel by driving off parasites that can't stand heat.[13]

As fall approaches, the grasses have dried out and much of the available seed has been consumed. Now the squirrels turn to the rich bounty of acorns falling from the oak trees. Acorns are important sustenance during lean times, but because of their high tannin content they are not an optimal diet. By late fall, most of the squirrels are spending a good deal of time below ground in their burrows. They will subsist on accumulated body fat and caches of acorns, expending the least amount of energy possible during the leanest part of the year.

Though they are an agricultural nuisance, in a *balanced* agricultural setting their damage is minimal.[14] Even fervent proponents for extermination realize that "the trouble and damage complained of (by ground squirrels) has come from agricultural communities where many people are fighting against the adversities of climate and pests on small tracts under not altogether favorable conditions."[15]

Looking at these animals as an integral, functioning part of a healthy landscape, one cannot help but marvel at their efficiency, a trait which modern man values highly. Undisturbed, the squirrels play a vital role in the balance of an ecosystem. They are a critical food source for various birds and reptiles, and experts at weed control. Their burrows aerate dense soils, while their accumulated litter, feces, and dead bodies nourish it. Their yearly life cycle dovetails perfectly with the cycles of the organisms they feed upon and with those which feed upon them. All of them dovetail perfectly with the larger climatic cycles of their environment. Round and round they go, perfectly adapted to their role in the world.

Over 100 years ago a naturalist traveling through California made the following prediction about California ground squirrels:

> Although difficult to exterminate, they will probably, in a few years, become as scarce in the settled districts as the Eastern squirrels now are in places where they formerly destroyed nearly all the crops, and had a premium placed on their heads.[15]

Fortunately, and despite the best of efforts, this has yet to happen.

Titmice and Magpies

AFTERNOON AND EVENING are blending; the worst heat of the day is over. A thin film of cloud Saran-wraps the eastern sky, trapping heat against the land. In lines from the north and south cows move toward the water trough. I nurse my cool beer accompanied by the faint sounds of little moving feet; a white-breasted nuthatch works its way around a branch, its feet clicking softly as it ferrets out insects from the bark. The birds are becoming active, taking advantage of the sweet respite between the long day's heat and the darkness of night. Two young bluebirds rest on the fence while a titmouse fusses in the branches overhead. A female bluebird joins the juveniles on the fence. She's the mother of these three kids and one of them begs at her shame-lessly.

From an oak tree far away, an acorn woodpecker makes its sawing-wood sound. The titmouse flutters out of the canopy to pick something off the ground. From an oak hurst to the east a flock of at least twenty magpies rises into the sky. They make a sinus-ey ruckus as they fly away in a long and crooked line.

Next to morning, this is the best time of the day. There is an almost palpable excitement as the birds feed and call noisily to each other. They claim their spaces for the night and re-establish ties and territories at the end of the day. The scientist in me knows it's not true, but the poet wants to believe the birds are singing their gratitude, relieved to have made it through another day, and excited about their prospects of making it through another night. As if to chide my silliness the titmouse engages in a barrage of raspy scoldings just above my head.

In his 1913 book on American birds Wheelock called the titmice (*Parus inornatus*) an "independent, aggressive little bird."[1] I heartily agree, and as long as I've given in to anthropomorphizing, I would add "loyal" to Wheelock's description. The mated pairs keep to themselves and their nest-rearing, doggedly attending to the business of providing for and protecting a family. They are independent in that they stay in the neighborhood year round. They don't fly off like the other birds once they have had their fill of seeds and bugs. Their presence is a reliable indication of the health of an oak woodland habitat and ecologists consider both titmice and yellow-billed magpies an indicator species: a species whose presence indicates a certain type of habitat.

The plain titmouse is certainly not a prepossessing little bird. In fact, the name "titmouse" is a jumbled redundancy of the Norse "tittr," meaning "small," and Anglo-Saxon "mase," meaning "small bird."[2] But for the conical crest perched atop its head like a miniature sorcerer's cap, there is little to visually distinguish this plain, grey bird. Its Latin name also indicates its stature; *Parus* stems from the Latin *parvus* for "small," and *inornatus* means "not ornate." Despite their rather Milquetoast appearance they are solid, capable defenders of the community, often the first to fuss noisily when danger approaches.

What they lack in physical appearance they make up for with their song. The plain titmouse has a variety of calls which can readily stump the unwary bird-watcher. During a bewildering excursion in Paso Robles, naturalist Bradford Torrey remarked:

> The titmice, indeed might almost have been called the birds of the day, their voices were so continually in my ears. Three times, at least, I heard what should have been a brand-new

bird, and each time the stranger turned out to be a plain tit rehearsing another tune. At the best he is only an indifferent singer, but his versatility is remarkable. He is one of the wise ones who make the most of a small gift.[3]

I've already confessed to anthropomorphizing titmice, but for complete catharsis I have to admit I do that with magpies too. I project the human virtues of tenacity, loyalty, and industriousness onto the titmice, but when it comes to human qualities like playfulness and mischievousness then my favorite birds are the yellow-billed magpies (*Pica nuttalli*).

When they teeter on a perch, with their garish yellow beaks and forlorn yellow-rimmed eyes, magpies look like they're imitating circus clowns. The way they strut around on the ground looks more like a bad John Wayne impersonation, and they are personable birds, calling to each other by name, "Mag? Mag?" My bird-watching friends don't share my amused fondness. Magpies are omnivores, eating seeds, insects, carrion, and frequently the eggs and chicks of songbirds. Because of the latter dainty they are unpopular with bird lovers.

But a yellow-billed magpie is a rare treasure. These birds exist only in the western shadow of the Sierra Nevada mountains.[4] They are endemic to this narrow range of central California and exist no where else in the world. I see them zigzagging across the pastel sky and I behold an evolutionary marvel. What happened thousands of years ago, among all the various magpie populations throughout the world, that here and only here, a yellow-billed species was produced?

Fossil records show that yellow-billed magpies existed at least 18,000 years ago.[5] At that point they co-existed in the southern half of California with black-billed magpies. Their bones were found together in the tar pits of Los Angeles and Carpintéria. Yet today black-billed magpies, though plentiful to the north and east of the Sierra Nevadas, are not found west or south. What changes happened, first to produce a separate species, and then to force the two species apart?

Did a climatic change cause a northern retreat among both species? North American magpies seem to have an affinity for more arid environments, so maybe precipitation increased at some point in the southernmost part of the state.[6] If so, did a larger population of yellow-bills just happen to retreat up the western side of the Sierra Nevadas and interbreed with black-bills until there were no more black-bill genes in their collective gene pool?

Black-billed magpies can tolerate greater cold than yellow-bills, while the latter has a greater heat tolerance.[7] Maybe some yellow-bills retreated along the eastern slopes then died out in the colder climate. Or maybe the other way around, with black-bills retreating up the western slopes and dying out in the stifling interior valleys.

And how *did* that darned yellow bill get into the population anyway? Did God just wake up one morning in central California and say to Himself, "God?—Yes?—I am sick unto death of looking at all these magpies with black bills. I think I'll make some of them yellow today.—Good idea." Simple enough, but not likely. Maybe out of millions of genes in millions of magpies, in just one bird, the gene that directs bill color may have simply miscoded. Instead of a black bill, a mutated yellow bill was produced.

I've done dozens of double-takes at yellow-billed magpies, thinking they were carrying a valley oak acorn in their beaks. They never were but at a quick glance it looks like they are. If I constantly think that a yellow-billed magpie is carrying around an acorn, imagine how the first black-billed birds reacted to that mutated yellow bill. Maybe they thought it was an acorn too. A bird like that, being such a consistent provider, would be a great mate. A bill that looked like a food offering would be of tremendous advantage in selecting a mate. It is what Darwin called a selective advantage: it confers an advantage to one bird over another. Like the difference between dating someone who drives an Escort and someone who drives a Mercedes.

That first yellow-billed bird might have been a very success-ful breeder. If so, it could have passed its mutated gene to its off-spring. Let's assume they all mated successfully because of this selective advantage and continued to pass the gene along. Over the course of time, the yellow-billed birds became firmly estab-lished within the black-billed population.

This is fun speculation but no one is sure how, where, or when the two species developed and diverged from each other. Except for the Roman poet Ovid.[8] He knew where the Euro-pean black-billed magpies came from.

According to Ovid, once there lived a wealthy Greek land-owner by the name of Pierus. He and his wife Euippe managed to produce nine daughters, no easy feat in the days before pre-natal care and organized medicine. These nine daughters were excessively proud of themselves and they roamed the Greek countryside vainly displaying their impressive multitude. One day the sisters arrived in the town of Helicon. This was the home of the Muses and the sisters promptly challenged the nine goddesses of song and poetry to a singing contest. The Muses initially felt it best to demure, but the challenge was so insult-ingly issued that it seemed worse to ignore it. The Muses agreed to the contest and river nymphs were chosen to be judges. One sister was chosen to represent all of Pierus' daughters, and one Muse was chosen to sing for all the Muses. When both of them finished their songs, the river nymphs busily conferred. They unanimously proclaimed the singer for the Muses the victor. The losing sisters were outraged. They piled insult after insult upon the Helicon goddesses until at last one of the Muses turned in a rage and cried, "Enough! First you come to our home and chal-lenge us to this ridiculous duel, and then when we win fairly you insult us. Our anger does have bounds and for this impudence you shall suffer."

So saying the Muse turned her back on the nine daughters of Pierus but even as they continued to taunt and tease the god-desses they saw themselves sprouting feathers and felt their noses hardening into beaks. Realizing what was happening they began to beat their breasts in despair. This only caused them to fly up into the air for the nine proud daughters were now nine new birds of the wood, the magpie. To this day they continue to call out to each other, "Mag? Mag?," as if still in disbelief that they are indeed magpies.

Mistletoe and the Druid

USK HAS CREPT STEALTHILY into the valley and is quietly defeating the day. The oaks are wrapped in twilight and the ridges lie salmon-colored in the dying blaze of the sun. As if in celebration the breeze has freshened, making the evening balmy, almost tropical.

For about thirty minutes I've been watching a coyote, probably the same one we saw this afternoon. It started off north by the herd of cows then circled behind the hill to come out on the east. I didn't see it come out from behind the hill and when I glanced up from my book there it was staring at me, with the big safety of the broad meadow between us. It dropped its head and moved on into the thick cover of the trees against the eastern ridge. About ten minutes later I saw it farther south and with another coyote. They casually slunk into a drainage and out of sight, but then I picked them up again as they made their way to the top of the ridge. They're paused there, one sitting and scratching, the other walking around sniffing. The salmon bleeds out of the hills and into the small clouds. I watch the coyotes as all the color fades from the landscape. Hill and cloud become the same murky, grey tone of dusk.

I can only see the coyotes now because their white throats make enough of a contrast against the darkening hills. They lounge on the ridge top and I yip at them, hopefully sounding like a coyote. Through my binoculars I see them look my way then slip over the other side of the ridge. Not the desired effect, but I am sure they will get even with me tonight when I am in the middle of a particularly fine dream.

I put the binoculars away and start a fire in my little barbecue kettle. It's not for warmth that I start the fire; like millions of ancestors before me, tonight I will sear animal flesh across the orange flames. When the small oak logs have burned down into hot coals I lay a strip of steak over them. I slice chunks off the steak, salt them down and chew them. I toss the fat to Mick and he grabs at it hungrily. With the fire gleaming in his eye he looks savage, like his lupine predecessors.

Sated, I lean back in my chair and let the night envelope me. With blood on my lips and fire in my eyes do I look savage too? I envision my Saxon and Celtic ancestors sacrificing a white bull to their panoply of demanding gods, flaying the beast at the alter to expose the rich flesh. Their sacrifices must not have been enough, for the culture of the Druidic peoples faded until only fragments of their mythology survived.

Darkness lunges against the orange coals. My imagination leaps as well, across centuries and continents, to the infamous "oak men" of old.[1] It is still debated today whether or not the Druids actually made human sacrifices to their gods, but it is well established that they did indeed worship spirits in the form of oak trees.[2]

I tend to think of Druids as an ancient sect of men in hooded cloaks restricted to the gloomy woods of the British Isles. In actuality, by 2,000 BC Druid culture was flourishing across the entire continent of Europe. Its full power would be realized a millennia and a half later.[3] The Druids were the priests of the Celtic peoples. They remain an obscure lot as much of Celtic mythology was committed to memory and shared only in the form of the spoken word. Written testament was distrusted among the Celts. All their sacred wisdom was kept in the hearts and minds of their priests. To become a Druid a man would train for up to twenty years. Established priests would then preside at all religious festivities and ceremonies, serving as mediators between Celtic gods councils, and individuals.[4]

Modern cultures tend to relegate God to churches and Sundays, but the ancient people's gods were directly tied to every facet of their daily lives. Their gods were alive in the clouds and trees above their heads. The rocks and serpents at their feet each had their own spirit. The deer and hare they hunted, the grain and herb they gathered, all were sacred beings. Very little could be done without direct supplication or acknowledgment to the myriad deities around them.[5] This animism, this belief that everything in the world surrounding them was alive and animated with a spirit, made the priests who were said to understand such spirits, and the requisite care and feeding of them, revered members of the society. The Druids could appease the gods that hurled thunder. They were the ones able to coax a stag to appear at the hunt. They knew how to please the gods living in the oak trees, and if the gods were pleased then the acorn crops would be plentiful. For the Celts, like the Salinans in our own backyards, were heavily reliant on the bounty of the plentiful oaks.[6]

That the Celts were able to occupy much of Europe, as dependent as they were upon the oak, suggests that at the time of their occupation oak forests were prevalent throughout the continent. This was true up into the late Dark Ages.[7] But while oak kingdoms remained in some spots, the Celtic kingdoms faded completely. Their power was weakened by Caesar's first century intrusions and inability to maintain cohesion among too many outposts too far from their Gaelic stronghold.

Caesar's observations offer rich nuggets of the little surviving information available about the Celts and their Druidic priesthood. It was he who called the Druids poets as well as priests, responsible as they were for passing on their rich history through oral form. As Christianity gained a foothold in the Celtic provinces, Druidic practices were outlawed. A second Druidic caste of diviners, called filidh, were allowed to tell the sacred, ancient poems unhampered. The telling of supernatural events (but not the *interpretation* of them, that was a Druid's imperative) was a function of a third caste, the bards. During the Christian take-over the bards were relegated to mere storytelling and entertaining. The word bard survived and is still used to describe a teller of epic poems.

With the Celts as with so many cultures around the world, a bountiful life and its continuance were ritually prayed for. Praying to an oak was an especially powerful form of prayer. Just as the Greeks at Dodona listened to the rustle of oak leaves, that they might divine a message from Zeus, so the Celts worshipped the oak.[8] Like the Greco-Romans, the Slavs, and the Norse, the Anglo-Saxons also believed that oaks were the favored earthly abodes of the lightning gods.

Every culture since time immemorial seems to have intuitively known that the sun is the ultimate giver of life. The Celts knew this too. They believed the blessings of the sun were passed on to the earth in the form of a brilliant and blinding lightning stroke. As oaks appeared to be the trees most frequently struck by lightning it would be natural for animistic cultures to believe that oaks were especially favored by the gods of lightning. To worship oaks was to curry favor with these all-powerful gods and their life-giving gifts.

One of these gifts was the mistletoe plant. The Celts believed that mistletoe was a tangible manifestation of their most powerful god, the sun. Because oaks were sacred, mistletoe found on them was considered even more potent than mistletoe found on other trees. But out of the literally thousands of plants that the Celts could have worshipped how did the inconspicuous mistletoe emerge as their *sine qua non*? Understanding its allure lies in understanding the organism itself.

The European mistletoe is *Viscum album* (literally "sticky white").[9] This is the mistletoe kissed under at Christmastime. A similar mistletoe grows on California oaks, the *Phoradendron* genus.[10] This is a not total parasite, but rather a partial or "hemi-parasite," which employs a host tree by the following method. Sticky mistletoe seeds are transported from tree to tree by birds. When lodged in place, the seeds extend a modified root under the bark of an oak branch. The *Phoradendron* root absorbs water and nutrients from its host and eventually conducts its own photosynthesis. Large amounts of this mistletoe may stress a tree but the *Phoradendron* rarely take so much that they kill their host. *Viscum* grows in a similar way.

Mistletoe must have awed the Celts. Sprouting as it does from the top of the tree rather than the ground, it seemingly has no roots or life-support systems. When oak leaves die in the winter, the mistletoe remains green. If squeezed, the mistletoe berries exude a sticky, white substance which bears somewhat of a resemblance to sperm. In addition, the mistletoe wood is a beautiful golden color much like the sun, hence its nickname, "the golden bough." All this led the ancient tree-worshipping people to believe that mistletoe was really the sun, placed on favored oak trees by powerful lightning gods.

To ingest mistletoe was to ingest the sun's strength and vigor. Bulls were also associated with vigor and fertility and when the Celts collected mistletoe they often sacrificed a bull in exchange. Mistletoe was considered an extremely powerful medicine, and was prescribed for any number of ailments from epilepsy to catatonia.[11] Its most important use may have been as a sacrifice: the plant was offered to the spirits, that they may grant fertility, be it in acorns, calves or people.

The idolatrous Celtic reverence of mistletoe vexed the conquering Christians. This antipathy is illustrated in a European folktale most likely generated as the incoming religion attempted to suppress the old. According to this story, mistletoe was a tree before the crucifixion of Jesus Christ. The pagans used it to make the sacrificial cross. Because of this, God changed the mistletoe into a parasite. From then on, it was humbly and forever reliant upon the support of others.[12]

Two Christmas traditions that still thrive today stem from the pagan beliefs of the Celts.[13] The endurance of these traditions testifies to the power and sway these people had over much of the western world.

At Christmas, it is common to hang mistletoe in doorways. When someone you desire walks through the door you kiss them. By continuing this ritual we still practice in the primal darkness of our subconscious the ancient fertility rites of our long-distant forebearers.

Yule logs are another Christmas tradition. Whether eaten symbolically as cakes or actually thrown on the fire, they are a remembrance of great pagan bonfires. In ritual commemoration of the winter solstice, which not coincidentally falls quite close to Christmas day, the Celts built enormous pyres. When Christian rulers outlawed pagan worship of the solstice, the bonfire celebration was brought indoors. During the celebration, a large, oaken log was burned on the hearth. Pieces of charcoal from this Yule log were then placed around the home to provide protection from lightning throughout the coming year. As the new religion supplanted the old, the Yule logs became smaller. The significance of the burning oak waned. Token logs were represented by Yule candles or cakes decorated in the shape of a log.

Today Christmas celebrations take many forms, but mistletoe and Yule log cakes (Buche d'Noel) still appear every year at this time. These are surviving links to our ancestral Druid kin. In these rituals, and sometimes, by dreaming in the livid glow of a fire's light, we yet pay homage to their memory.

Scorpio

THE OAK COALS wink like small eyes under hoods of grey ash. Far off a great horned owl hoots softly. Somewhere the coyotes are hunting and some small creature will not live through the night.

I unroll the sleeping bag in the back of the truck, my head out on the tailgate. The whole night sky dangles above me, a drawn theater curtain sprinkled with silver glitter. Having traveled across the sky all day, the thin moon is already spent and the stars take center stage. To the south I see Scorpio crawling against the horizon. This is my favorite summer constellation because it is one of the few that actually looks like its name; even the ancient Persians and Egyptians called this constellation a scorpion.[1] Antares, the brightest star in this constellation, gleams at the head of the scorpion like an omnipotent eye.[2] The temperature on this star is a fiery 3,100 degrees Celsius, and like the planet Mars, it too has a distinctly reddish glow.[3]

In summer, Scorpio is the most recognizable cluster of stars, but in the winter I can easily find the Orion constellation. It stands out against the northern sky as a brightly belted warrior. Orion, as you may recall from Roman mythology lessons, was an extremely proficient hunter. He was so good he even impressed Diana, goddess of the hunt. Orion impressed himself too, and he boasted frequently that no animal was safe from his deadly aim. Evidently Juno, up high in her heavens one day, grew weary of Orion's braggadocio. Promptly she devised a way to silence him.

The next morning, as Orion trode the usual path to his hunting grounds, a tiny insect stung the mighty hunter upon his heel. Instantly Orion collapsed in a lifeless heap. The great Orion had been felled by a lowly scorpion. Moved by love, Diana begged Jupiter to place Orion's body in the sky, that she might see him every night. Jupiter consented, but when Juno learned of this she demanded that the scorpion be placed in the firmaments as well. Again Jupiter consented, but in order to keep heavenly peace he wisely placed Orion in the north and the scorpion in the south. Thus the two rivals rise at separate times of the year, their paths never crossing.[4]

I snuggle my head back into the bag, reassured that the ancient heavens are still boldly and beautifully looking down upon me. But not only me, for this starry light has shined upon countless others. Light from these stars rested on the heads of Socrates and Pliny. The women in the valleys of the Middle East planted seed under the watchful eye of this Zodiac. Jesus and the *paganorum* wandered below this glimmering sky. Passenger pigeons once migrated against these stars. Spanish soldiers followed the path of these constellations across the seas and into these valleys. Druidic priests left their prayerful offerings for the sun which always turned and hid its face into the night. Unmoved, these stars looked down upon the dark-running altars.

All those people existed. They once moved and thought and felt, just as I move and think and feel tonight. The stars saw them just as they see me now. The stars watched those people die, and they will watch me die someday too. I will take part in that most dependable and reliable of all cycles. People are ephemeral, but the stars will remain. That I have witnessed them is like leaving a small part of myself up there to live on.

I have came to the valley as Lao-tzu instructed and I have used its spirit. The valley has burned me and its shade has cooled me. Its silence has emptied me and its song has filled me. Its earth has held me and its sky has released me. I close my eyes and dream. I am in the pounding heart of eternity, somewhere between heaven and earth.

Epilogue

THE RICE IS THROWN, the bouquet tossed, the bride and groom gone in a clatter of tin cans. The scientist and the poet are wed.

On their honeymoon in Yosemite National Park the scientist saw fence lizards and meticulously categorized them as *Sceloporus occidentalis*. But on closer examination, she realized they were slightly different than western fence lizards. The differences were slight, but they were enough for her field guide to classify them as a subspecies, the Sierra fence lizard, *Sceloporus occidentalis taylori*. The scientist reduced the lizards to as individual an essence as she could.

The poet saw a lizard basking on a cliff face and had no idea what its Latin name was. But instead of seeing individual distinctions he recognized the lizard as a universal symbol. Through his knowledge of art and literature, history and mythology, he remembered a shared, cultural affinity for this animal. That day he wrote a poem, and in it he mentioned a lizard skittering over a golden wall. He used the lizard to represent regeneration and recreation.

Where the scientist reduced an organism to its finite definition, the poet broadened it to encompass a cosmologic function. Later that evening, sitting by the yellow warmth of the fire and sharing a glass of wine, they told each other what they had done during the day.

The scientist said calmly, "I saw Sierra fence lizards this morning. I was so excited, because even though they're related to the fence lizards we have at home, they're still a unique subspecies that you can only see in the Sierras."

"Really?" exclaimed the poet. "I didn't know they were different. I saw some lizards too and they inspired me to write a poem!"

The scientist was puzzled. "Why would lizards inspire you to write a poem?"

"Because they represent sunshine, and renewal. Cultures all around the world see them as a symbol of regeneration. And here it is summer, and everything's growing and renewing itself and they so personified that for me."

The scientist thoughtfully sipped her wine and commented, "I see. They probably symbolize regeneration because they can grow new tails."

"No way!"

"It's true. If they lose their old tail they can grow a new one."

"I didn't know that," marveled the poet.

"And I didn't know they symbolized the sun."

In this marriage between science and mythology each partner will share knowledge. Each will learn from the other. They round out the rough edges and fill in the holes where the other lacks ideas. The heart of the poet and the mind of the scientist merge. By sharing their stories, they grow. They become whole.

Within this work, the ecology of the landscape has been woven into its mythology and its stories. Each organism encountered is perfectly and uniquely adapted to its role in this landscape. Mythologies tend to overlook or ignore these adaptations, disregarding the centuries of effort behind their creation. In ignoring these subtle adaptations humans risk upsetting a chain of events that have been in process far longer than we have been on earth. By altering this balance, humans imperil their own existence. We depend on the earth's continuity for our own.

Likewise we depend on the continuity of our stories, our mythologies, our epic poems. They hold the words that keep our hearts alive. When asked why he was writing a book about bird folk-lore, Edward Armstrong said this:

> No community which loses its sense of continuity with the past can be socially and spiritually healthy, nor can institutions be intelligently reformed without a knowledge of their history. Tradition has sometimes become the dead hand of the past on the present but this is not our danger today. Many are so far from overvaluing the past as to be unaware that they belong to any ancient tradition. Technological advance and the new ways of thinking which accompany it menace the good life unless new knowledge is integrated with the old. Perhaps this study, by calling attention to the significance of a neglected aspect of our heritage, may encourage, not merely an academic interest in ancient things still present with us, but the personal identification with tradition which gives a community strength and has so often been the inspiration of saints, patriots, poets and musicians, as well as a solace and delight, accepted almost as unconsciously as the air they breathe, by simple folk.[1]

Science and mythology have long been at loggerheads, the proponents of each powerfully trying to force the other to accept its viewpoint. Belief in epic stories rests purely on faith. Belief in science rests solely on proof. But proof has been known to fail as easily as faith. Neither extreme is healthy. A lesson from looking at the landscape should be obvious—there has to be compromise. Paradoxically, a continuously shifting, fluxing state of balance between all parts of the landscape usually yields the most stable, sustainable outcome. Maintaining a balanced community is like standing alone on the middle of a see-saw, it is a constant dance from left foot to right in order to remain centered. The scientist who understands the mythological roots of the organism she studies is a richer scientist, just as the poet who understands a few scientific principles about the organisms he describes is a richer poet.

Their viewpoints are different yet equal. Each partner offers their own unique values to the relationship and sets up the dynamic in which creation is possible. And so it is with the wedding of science to mythology. Together they dance in the center of the see-saw. Together they are whole. May the marriage be long and blessed.

Notes

Introduction—The Valley

1. Poem 6, from Lao-tzu (1962), p. 110, is:

> The spirit of the valley never dies.
> It is called the subtle and profound female.
> The gate of the subtle and profound female
> Is the root of Heaven and Earth.
> It is continuous, and seems to be always existing.
> Use it and you will never wear it out.

Wing-tsit Chan, who translated this volume, feels that this is not a supernatural meaning for the spirit of the valley (see Blakney) but a more organic interpretation. He feels that Lao-tzu refers to the valley's spirit as something continually undergoing change and regeneration.

Chapter 1—California

1. No one is exactly certain how California got its name, but this is a widely accepted theory started by Hale in 1872. See Hale, E.E. (1968).

2. Capturing condor chicks is mentioned by Beals and Hester (1974), Kroeber (1925), and Simons (1983).

3. See Hittell (1885).

4. In addition to Hittell (1885), Richman (1965) is a good source for information about Cortés.

5. See Schoenherr (1992). This, and Bakker (1971), are excellent introductory guides to California ecology.

Chapter 2—Biophilia

1. Brewer (1949), p. 92.

2. See Wilson (1984). Scientists write so many books, but very few of them are fun to read. Wilson writes easily and disarmingly about provocative subjects.

3. Lumsden and Wilson (1983), p. 60.

4. Lumsden and Wilson (1981), p. 1.

5. See Ulrich (1993).

6. See Richardson (1972) and Wilson (1984, 1993).

7. Some cultures venerate dangerous animals such as snakes. According to Wilson (1984, 1993), Lawrence (1993), Nelson (1993) and Ulrich (1993) this is a way to safely cope with the fear and mystery surrounding these animals.

8. See Appleton (1975), Heerwagen and Orians (1993) and Ulrich (1993).

9. Ibid.

10. Lawrence (1993), p. 332.

11. Appleton (1975), p. 169.

Chapter 3—Steinbeck

1. Steinbeck was extremely well-read. This literacy surfaced throughout his many works. The mythologies he wove in and around his story lines varied from Christian bible myths to Hindu and Taoist legends, from the ancient pantheism of Frazer's *Golden Bough* to the more modern Arthurian and Shakespearean tales. Steinbeck had a poetic nature, yet at the same time an avid respect for and appreciation of the natural world. This was also incorporated into his works. He relied heavily on natural elements for symbolism and knew enough science to accompany Ed Ricketts on a data gathering ocean journey. From that trip Ricketts and another colleague co-authored a premiere California marine biology text, *Between Pacific Tides*. Steinbeck ably wrote the introduction to this manual, which is still in common use today.

2. As a child, Steinbeck lived in the city of Salinas. His maternal grandparents lived roughly ten miles south of King City, and his paternal grandparents lived near Fremont Peak, just south of San Juan Bautista.

3. Steinbeck (1952), p. 2-3.

4. Wilson (1993), p. 32.

5. Steinbeck (1975), p. 24.

Chapter 4—Annual Grasses

1. See Davies and Hillman (1992).

2. For excellent histories of grass domestication see the above, de Wet (1992), Harlan (1992), Sauer (1993) and Zohary and Hopf (1993).

Chapter 5—More Annual Grasses

1. Ibid. Also Hendry (1931) and Spencer (1957).

2. See Burcham (1982).

3. See Bancroft (1963a), Burcham (1982) and Richman (1965).

4. Ibid.

5. Wilson (1984), p. 19.

Chapter 6—Bluebirds and Sky

1. Earwigs were named after the erroneous superstition that they had a penchant for worming their way into people's ears—hence the suffix "wig," from the Old English *wicga*, meaning "worm." See Langston and Powell (1975).

2. See Fox (1976), Simon (1971) and Welty and Baptista (1988).

3. Before anthropomorphism became a cardinal scientific sin, many natural history writers incorporated the creativity of a poet with the observational skills of a scientist. Chapman (1930), Coues (1894), Dawson (1923), Forbush (1939), and Pearson (1936) are fine examples of this style.

4. Dawson (1923), p. 778.

Chapter 7—Going Native

1. For grass biology see Bakker (1971), Beetle (1947), Biswell (1956), Crampton (1974),Evans and Young (1972) and Jain (1972).

2. See Borror (1960).

3. See Appendix A.

4. The missing three are the Oregon, Englemann, and Island Oaks. See Griffin and Critchfield (1976).

5. See Griffin (1973) and Jepson (1910).

6. See Bancroft (1963b), Costanso (1911), Font (1933) and Palou (1926).

7. I briefly site some of the major reasons for declining California oak populations. For in-depth analysis of these reasons (in the order presented in the text) see the following: Rossi (1979, 1980); Duncan and Clawson (1980), Holland (1973, 1980), Holland and Morton (1980); Muick and Stewart (1992), Roberts and Smith (1980); Danielson and Halvorson (1991), Griffin (1971), Gordon, Welker, Mencke and Rice (1989), Holland (1976).

8. That statistic is for 1995 according to the World Book of Facts (1997).

9. See Kuhn-Schnyder and Rieber (1986). 45,000 years represents evolution of the modern species of mountain lion.

10. It is currently illegal to hunt mountain lions in California. This protection appears to have boosted lion population numbers. The ensuing increase is a boon to the natural ecology but exacerbates conflicts with humans. Continued protection of these animals is a highly-charged issue.

11. Wilson (1984), p. 121.

Chapter 8—Acorns

1. See Breschini (1983a, 1983b) and Kroeber (1925) for geographical distribution of Native Americans throughout the central coast inlands.

2. The tanbark is a close relative of the true oaks, in the genus *Lithocarpus*.

3. This story comes from Pavlik (1991) who cites his source as John P. Harrington, *Bureau of American Ethnography Bulletin No. 7*, 1932.

4. See Chartkoff and Chartkoff (1984).

5. See Costanso (1911) and Palou (1926).

6. See Beals and Hester (1974), Chestnut (1902), Mayer (1976) and Merriam (1918).

7. Ibid. See also Ebeling (1986).

8. See Bainbridge (1986), Baumhoff (1963) and Merriam (1918).

9. See Abrams (1923) and Jepson (1910).

10. Based on Mayer (1976).

11. See Appendix B.

Chapter 9—Acorn Woodpeckers

1. See Johnson (1984).

2. See Gruson (1972).

3. For food habits of acorn woodpeckers see MacRoberts (1970, 1974), Ritter (1938) and Winkler, Christie and Nurney (1995).

4. See Winkler, Christie and Nurney (1995).

5. See Bock (1964), May (1976) and Winkler, Christie and Nurney (1995).

6. See Cronise (1868) and MacRoberts (1974).

7. See Pliny (1967), p. 581.

8. See Bergier (1941).

9. See McCulloch (1962) and White (1954).

10. See Armstrong (1970), Grimm (1966), Kelly (1969) and Thiselton-Dyer (1971).

Chapter 10—Early Biology

1. Sarton's works are exhaustive and require more time than someone with a casual interest in scientific history may care to spend. A far more succinct (and equally enjoyable) accounting is written by Moore (1993). During my academic career this was the only required-reading textbook from which I ever read chapters ahead of their assigned date.

2. See Clair (1967), Clark and McMunn (1989), McCulloch (1962), Metropolitan Museum of Art, New York (1965), *Physiologus* (1979) and Rowland (1989).

3. The original *Physiologus* was a Greek work written in the 2nd century as a naturalist's guide. Later it was translated into Latin, and edited with the inclusion of moralistic teachings by 4th century Romans.

4. See Bartlett (1982).

5. Ibid.

6. *Physiologus* (1979), p. 27.

Chapter 11—San Joaquin Kit Fox

1. See Carey (1982) and Waters (1964).

2. For kit fox distribution see Grinnell, Dixon and Linsdale (1937), Laughrin (1970) and Orloff, Hall and Spiegel (1986).

3. See Dragoo, Choate, Yates and O'Farrell (1990), Kurten and Anderson (1980), and Mercure, Ralls, Koepfli and Wayne (1993) for evolutionary history.

4. See Balestreri (1981), Logan, Berry, Standley and Kato (1992) and O'Farrell (1987).

5. In their 1986 report, Orloff, Hall and Spiegel also mention this switch in prey preference in the kit fox's northern-most range.

Chapter 12—5052

1. In 1988, 103 individual kit foxes were captured with the same trapping methods we currently use. In 1991 that number had declined to 20. No trapping was conducted in 1992, but the following year only 17 individual foxes were captured. That number jumped to 31 animals in 1994 then fell again and in 1996 only 9 individual kit foxes were caught.

Chapter 13—Lightning

1. See Eagleman (1983), Marshall (1983) and Uman (1987).

2. Ibid. See also Lee (1977).

3. See Golde (1977) and Schonland (1964).

4. See Berger (1977), Marshall (1983).

5. See Carruthers (1972), Leach (1950) and Frazer (1981).

6. See Golde (1973) and Taylor (1977).

7. The word "smithereen" is passed down from the Old Irish "smiderin," meaning "fragment."

8. See Schonland (1964) and Taylor (1977).

9. Per a 1993 Weather Service report for 1991. See Weather Service Headquarters (1993).

10. See Dibner (1977), Eagleman (1983) and Schonland (1964).

Chapter 14—Western Fence Lizards

1. The older name for this suborder, Lacertilia, was more fun. From the Latin word for the bicep muscle, *lacerta*, it meant to ripple on the arm, much as a lizard ripples across the ground. See White (1954) and Oxford English Dictionary (1961).

2. Populations of Western fence lizards with slight distinctions are found in specific locations throughout California. These are *Sceloporus occidentalis* too, but based on their distinctions they are given sub-species names. For example, the Sierra fence lizard found only above 7,000 feet in the Sierra Nevada range is *Sceloporus occidentalis taylori*.

3. See Richardson (1972) and Smith (1946).

4. Leach (1950), p. 637.

5. See Bayley (1974), Gubernatis (1968), Topsell (1967) and White (1954). According to Topsell and Bayley the name *lacerta* also signifies "shining light."

6. White (1954), p. 184.

7. Regeneration sometimes occurs when the tail is only partially severed, thus creating a forked tailed. See Smith (1946).

8. I find it interesting that we call someone repellent a "creep" and the word "reptile" means "creeping" in Latin.

Chapter 15—Datura

1. See Duke (1985), Heiser (1969) and Schleiffer (1973).

2. Moore (1979), p. 92. A number of years ago I took a weekend class with Michael Moore. He knows his plants and he knows their effects as he has

tried almost all of the remedies he prescribes. Unlike many herbalists he doesn't hold to the "body as temple" philosophy. He will easily down a greasy burger and fries with a pitcher of beer, so his remedies for heartburn and hangovers are as tried and true as his remedies for more esoteric complaints.

3. For medicinal information about scopolamine and its sister alkaloids check Duke (1985), Haggard (1929), Heiser (1969), Moore (1979), Osol, Pratt and Gennaro (1973) and Taylor (1965).

4. See Osol, Pratt and Gennaro (1973).

5. See Schultes (1979) and Schultes and Hofmann (1973).

6. Dioscorides (1959), p. 470.

7. Ibid, p. 473.

8. See Schleiffer (1979), Schultes and Hofmann (1973), Seligman (1948) and Siegel (1984).

9. This old faith was called the *religio paganorum* or "religion of the villagers." From the Latin *pagus* for "villager," comes the term "pagan," denoting someone who believes in a religion other than Christianity.

10. Donaldson (1994), Inglis (1965) and Singer (1958).

11. Scapegoat is an appellation drawn quite literally from a Latin translation of the Hebrew, "desert demon."

12. Brown (1971), Hansen (1976), Jacobs (1965, 1967) and Singer (1958).

13. Brown (1971), Haggard (1929) and Kingsbury (1965).

14. le Strange (1977), p. ix.

15. Donaldson (1994), Haggard (1929) and Inglis (1965).

16. Harmon (1992), p. 368.

Chapter 16—Band-Tailed Pigeons

1. See Goodwin (1977) and Levi (1957).

2. See Levi (1957).

3. See Bulfinch (1962), Graves (1942), MacCulloch (1962) and Rowland (1968).

4. As with most flocking birds, especially during the breeding season, there is bound to be some aggressive interactions between males vying for females. In captivity this aggressive behavior often goes unchecked. In an enclosure a subordinate male cannot leave a dominant male's territory. It is instinctual for the dominant male to try and force his attacker to flee, and it does not know the weaker fellow can't escape—it only knows it's still in his territory and it's a pigeon's job to defend this space. In the wild the weaker male would most likely fly away before the stronger male could even get a good peck at it.

5. For general pigeon biology see Dock (1979), Edminster (1954), Leopold (1948) and Mallette (1987).

6. Pigeon mating reminds me of a curious piece of genetics history. A prevailing Medieval belief was that what females saw while they copulated influenced what their offspring would look like. As a result pigeon owners would only put their most beautiful birds together during mating time so that the females could only look upon other gorgeous creatures, thus producing only beautiful offspring.

7. See Dalrymple (1949) and Schorger (1955).

8. See Edminster (1954) and Smith (1968).

9. See Holy Bible, Book of Ecclesiastes, Chapter 1 and 2 especially.

Chapter 17—Oak Galls and Gall Wasps

1. See Russo (1979).

2. See Felt (1940) and Russo (1979).

3. See Askew (1984) and Weld (1957).

4. See Dailey and Sprenger (1973) and Wiebes-Rijks and Shorthouse (1992).

5. The word parthenogenesis stems from the Greek *partheno* and *genesis*, meaning respectively "virgin" and "origin." In Greece, the Parthenon was erected in honor of their virgin goddess Athena. After Christianity supplanted the Greek deities in the 6th century, the Parthenon was dedicated to Mary, the virgin mother.

6. See Askew (1984), Felt (1940), Weld (1957) and Wiebes-Rijks and Shorthouse (1992).

7. See Robbins, et al (1987a) and Robbins, et al (1987b).

Chapter 18—California Ground Squirrels

1. See Thiselton-Dyer (1968).

2. See Borror (1960).

3. See Beechey (1831).

4. See Kroeber (1925).

5. In her 1980 Master's thesis Edwina Smith concisely details the eradication history of the California ground squirrel. Here I have briefly outlined her account, but I heartily recommend reading her entire thesis if you have more interest in these animals than I have satisfied here.

6. Ibid.

7. Ibid.

8. Ibid.

9. See Schitoskey (1973).

10. See Appendix C.

11. See Fitch (1948), Linsdale (1946) and Schitoskey (1973).

12. See Topsell (1967) and Toynbee (1973).

13. See Linsdale (1946) and Schitoskey (1973).

14. See Grinnell (1923), Heady and Child (1994).

15. See Smith (1980), p. 274

16. Cronise (1868), p. 443.

Chapter 19—Titmice and Magpies

1. Wheelock (1913), p. 348.

2. See Choate (1973), Gruson (1972) and Swann (1968).

3. Torrey (1913), p. 116.

4. See Linsdale (1937) and Robbins, Bruun and Zim (1983).

5. See Linsdale (1937), Lundelius, et al (1983), and Miller (1932, 1937).

6. See Reynolds (1995).

7. See Birkhead (1991), Linsdale (1937) and Reynolds (1995).

8. See Ovid, (1955).

Chapter 20—Mistletoe and the Druids

1. "Druid" stems from the Gaelic *duir* for "oak" and *wyd* for "men."

2. The oak trees of the British isles were of the *robur* species, "robust" in Latin.

3. See MacCana (1970) and Spence (1971).

4. Celtic history is well-researched by MacCana (1970), MacCulloch (1911), Ross (1967) and Spence (1971). Graves (1942) dealt with it from a poets perspective and Caesar (1884) contributed many observations of the Celtic people during his incursions into the British Isles.

5. See Frazer (1981) and Grimm (1966) as well as above authors.

6. The German mythologist Grimm traces the origin of the Latin word for acorn, *juglans*, from *Jovis glans*, Jove's (Jupiter's) glands. This literally means "fruit of the father," bearing testimony to the sanctity of the acorn.

7. See Hehn and Stallybrass (1888), MacCulloch (1911) and Spence (1971).

8. See Baring-Gould (1967), Bayley (1974), Goldsmith (1973) and Porteous (1968).

9. For mistletoe biology see Calder (1983) and Hawksworth (1983).

10. Another common California mistletoe is the *Arceuthobium*. This species prefers conifers and unlike the Phoradendron often causes extensive damage to the host tree.

11. See Calder (1983), Pliny (1967), Spence (1971) and Thiselton-Dyer (1968).

12. See Baring-Gould and Porteous (1928).

13. See Miles (1976).

Chapter 21—Scorpio

1. See Burnham (1978), Lum (1948) and Webb (1952).

2. In mythology, Mars and Antares are celestial rivals. The ancient Greeks called Mars "Ares," hence the name *Ant-ares*, meaning opposite-Ares.

3. See Burnham (1978) and Hathaway (1994).

4. See Lum (1948), Webb (1952) and Proctor (1972).

Epilogue

1. See Armstong (1970).

California Oak Species

California oaks freely hybridize within their own subgenus. The following list does not include hybrid species; only parent species native to California are included here. For a comprehensive treatment of hybrid species see Tucker (1980).

WHITE OAKS

1. *Quercus douglassi*—Blue Oak
2. *Quercus dumosa*—Scrub Oak
3. *Quercus durata*—Leather Oak
4. *Quercus engelmannii*—Engelmann Oak, Mesa Oak
5. *Quercus garryana*—Oregon Oak
6. *Quercus lobata*—Valley Oak
7. *Quercus sadleriana*—Deer Oak
8. *Quercus turbinella*—Desert Scrub Oak

INTERMEDIATE OAKS

9. *Quercus chrysolepis*—Canyon Live Oak, Maul Oak
10. *Quercus palmeri*—Palmer Oak, Dunn Oak
11. *Quercus tomentella*—Island Oak
12. *Quercus vaccinifolia*—Huckleberry Oak

BLACK OAKS

13. *Quercus agrifolia*—Coast Live Oak

14. *Quercus kelloggii*—Black Oak
15. *Quercus wislizenii*—Interior Live Oak

Per Tucker (1980) and Muick and Stewart (1992), the three subgenera of the genus *Quercus* are white oaks (*Lepidobalanus*), black oaks (*Erythrobalanus*) and intermediate oaks (*Protobalanus*).

Acorn Caloric Values

Based on Mayer's calculations I averaged the average daily caloric intake of a family of six (two pre-adolescents at 2,000 calories each, two adolescents at 2,800 calories each and two adults at 3,000 calories each) to get an average daily calorie need of 15,600. Multiply that by 365 days per year and a family of six would need 5,694,000 calories per year.

Again based on Mayer's calculations, a pound of acorns provides an average of 2,718 calories. Therefore a family of six would need 5,694,000 kcal/2,718 kcal or 2,094 pounds of acorns per year.

Caloric Needs of Adult California Ground Squirrels

Schitoskey's (1973) formula for estimating daily caloric needs is as follows:

He estimates an adult male ground squirrel weighing 668 grams needs to consume 61,117 calories per day. He divided calories needed per day by the amount of calories per gram of green forage (4650) to get 13.15 grams of forage needed per day.

Because only 49% of that matter is digested he used a conversion coefficient of 0.397 (see below) divided into the 13.15 grams needed daily to arrive at 32.9 grams of forage needed daily.

The conversion coefficient is (0.49)(0.90)(0.90), 0.49 being percent of food that is actually metabolizable (his word), 0.90 being the percent of food remaining after its conversion to metabolizable energy, and the other 0.90 being percent of food remaining after the metabolizable energy is converted to net energy.

The same formula was used to obtain the daily caloric needs of a seed diet.

References

Abrams, L. (1923.) *Illustrated flora of the Pacific States* (Vol. 1.) Stanford: Stanford University.

Armstrong, E. A. (1970). *The folklore of birds: an enquiry into the origin and distribution of some magico-religious traditions.* New York: Dover Publications.

Appleton, J. (1975). *The experience of landscape.* London: Wiley.

Askew, R.R. (1984). The biology of gall wasps. In T.N. Ananthakrishnan (Ed.), *The biology of gall insects* (pp. 223-272). London: Edward Arnold.

Bainbridge, D.A. (1986.) The use of acorns for food in California, past, present, future. In: Plumb, T.R. and N. Pillsbury (Eds.). *Proceedings of the symposium on multiple-use management of California's hardwood resources* (pp. 453-458). Berkeley, CA: U.S. Department of Agriculture. Forest Service Pacific Southwest and Range Experiment Station.

Balestreri, A.N. (1981.) *Status of the San Joaquin kit fox at Camp Roberts, California, 1981.* Department of the Army, Fort Ord, California, Contract No. DAKF03-81-M-C736. 48pp.

Bakker, E. (1971.) *An island called California.* Berkeley: University of California Press.

Bancroft, H.H. (1963a). *The works of Hubert Howe Bancroft: Volume XVIII. History of California: Vol. I 1542-1800:* (Introd. Edmund G. Brown).Santa Barbara: Wallace Hebberd. (Original work published 1886.)

Bancroft, H.H. (1963b). *The works of Hubert Howe Bancroft: Volume XVIII. History of California: Vol. II 1801-1824:* (Introd. Edmund G. Brown). Santa Barbara: Wallace Hebberd. (Original work published 1886.)

Baring-Gould, E. (1967). *Curious myths of the Middle Ages.* New York: University Books.

Bartlett, J. (1982). *Familiar quotations* (13th ed.). Boston: Little, Brown. (Original work published 1882.)

Baumhoff, M.A. (1963). Ecological determinants of aboriginal California populations. *University of California Publications in American Archeology and Ethnology,* **49** (2), 155-235.

Bayley, H. (1974). *The lost language of symbolism: An inquiry into the origin of certain letters, words, names, fairy-tales, folklore and mythologies.* London: Rowan and Littlefield. (Originally published in 1912.)

Beals, R.L. & Hester, J.A., Jr. (1974). *Indian occupancy, subsistence, and land use patterns in California.* New York: Garland.

Beechey, F.W. (1831). *Narrative of a voyage to the Pacific and Bering's Strait in the years 1825, '26, '27, '28,* (Vol. II). London: Henry Colburn and Richard Bentley.

Beetle, A.A. (1947). Distribution of the native grasses of California. *Hilgardia,* **17,** 309-357.

Berger, K. (1977). The earth flash. In R.H. Golde (Ed.), *Lightning* (Vols. 1-2) (pp. 119-190). New York: Academic Press.

Bergier, E. (1941). *Peuples entomophages et insectes comestibles.* Avignon: Imprimerie Rulliere Freres.

Birkhead, T.R. (1991). *The magpies: The ecology and behaviour of black-billed and yellow-billed magpies.* London: T & AD Poyser.

Biswell, H.H. (1956). Ecology of California grasslands. *Journal of Range Management,* **9,** 19-24.

Bock, W.J. (1964). Kinetics of the avian skull. *Journal of Morphology,* **114,** 1-41.

Borror, D. J. (1960). *Dictionary of word roots and combining forms.* Palo Alto: N-P Publishing.

Breschini, G.S. (1983a). *Models of population movements in Central California prehistory.* Salinas: Coyote Press.

Breschini, G.S. (1983b). *A cultural resources overview of the Coastal and Coast Valley Study Area.* Salinas: Coyote Press.

Brewer, W.H. (1949). *Up and down California in 1860-1864: The journal of William H. Brewer* (2nd ed.) (Francis P. Farquhar, Ed.). Berkeley: University of California Press.

Brown, R.L. (1971). *A book of witchcraft.* New York: Taplinger.

Bulfinch, T. (1962). *The age of fable: Or beauties of mythology.* New York: New American Library. (Original work published 1855.)

Burcham, L.T. (1982). *California range land: An historico-ecological study of the range resource of California.* (Introd. G. James West). Davis: University of California. (Original work published 1957.)

Burnham, R., Jr. (1978). *Burnham's celestial handbook: An observer's guide to the universe beyond the solar system* (Vol. 3). New York: Dover.

Calder, D.M. (1983). Mistletoe in focus. In Malcolm Clader & Peter Bernhardt (Eds.), *The biology of mistletoes* (pp. 1-18). North Ryde, Australia: Academic Press.

Caesar. 1884. *Caesar's commentaries.* (J. Hamilton & T. Clark, Trans.). Philadelphia: David McKay.

Carey, A.B. (1982). The ecology of red foxes, gray foxes, and rabies in the eastern United States. *Wildlife Society Bulletin,* **10,** 18-26.

Carruthers, Miss, of Inverness. (1972). *Flower lore.* Detroit: Singing Tree Press. (Original work published in 1879.)

Chapman, F.M. (1930). *Birdlife: A guide to the study of our common birds.* New York: D. Appleton.

Chartkoff, J. L. and K. K. Chartkoff. (1984). *The archaeology of California.* Stanford, California: Stanford University Press.

Chestnut, V.K. (1902). Plants used by the Indians of Mendocino County, California. *U.S. National Museum Contributions to the U.S. National Herbarium,* **7,** 295-408.

Choate, E.A. (1973). *The dictionary of American bird names.* Boston: Gambit.

Clair, C. (1967). *Unnatural history.* London and New York: Abelard-Schuman.

Clark, W.B. and M.T McMunn. (1989). Introduction. In W.B. Clark & M.T. McMunn (Eds.) *Beasts and birds of the Middle Ages: The bestiary and its legacy* (pp. 1-11). Philadelphia: University of Pennsylvania Press.

Costanso, M. 1911. *The Portola expedition of 1769-1770: Diary of Miguel Costanso.* (F.J. Teggart, Ed.). Berkeley: University of California.

Coues, E. (1894). *Key to North American birds* (4th ed.). Boston: Estes & Lauriat.

Crampton, B. (1974). *Grasses in California*. Berkeley: University of California Press.

Cronise, T.F. (1868). *The natural wealth of California*. San Francisco: H.H. Bancroft.

Dailey, D.C. & C.M. Sprenger. (1973). Unisexual generation of *Andricus-Atrimentus. Pan-Pacific Entomologist,* **49** (2), 171-173.

Dalrymple, B.W. (1949). *Doves and dove shooting*. New York: G.P. Putnam's Sons.

Danielsen, K.C. and W.L. Halvorson. (1991). Valley oak seedling growth associated with selected grass species. In Standiford, Richard B. Ed.), *Proceedings of the symposium on oak woodlands and hardwood rangeland management* (pp. 9-13). Berkeley: Pacific Southwest Research Station, Forest Service, U.S. Department of Agriculture.

Davies, M.S. & G.C. Hillman. (1992). Domestication of cereals. In G. P. Chapman (Ed.), *Grass evolution and domestication* (pp. 199-224). Cambridge: Cambridge University Press.

Dawson, W.L. (1923). *The birds of California: A complete, scientific and popular account of the 580 species and subspecies of birds found in the state* (Vol. 2). San Diego: South Moulton.

de Wet, J.M.J. (1992). The three phases of cereal domestication. In G. P. Chapman (Ed.), *Grass evolution and domestication* (pp. 176-198). Cambridge: Cambridge University Press.

Dibner, B. (1977). Benjamin Franklin. In R.H. Golde (Ed.), *Lightning* (Vols. 1-2) (pp. 23-50) New York: Academic Press.

Dioscorides. (1959). *The Greek herbal of Dioscorides* (Intro. Robert T. Gunther). (2nd ed). New York: Hafner. (Original work published 1 AD.)

Dock, G. (1979). *Audubon's birds of America*. New York: Harry N. Abrams.

Donaldson, D.D. (1994, May). Lecture series presented in *History of Biology*, California Polytechnic University, San Luis Obispo.

Dragoo, J.W., J.R. Choate, T.L.Yates and O'Farrell, T.P. (1990). Evolutionary and taxonomic relationships among North American arid-land foxes. *Journal of Mammalogy,* **71** (3), 318-332.

Duke, J.A. (1985). *Handbook of medicinal herbs*. Boca Raton: CRC Press.

Duncan, D.A. & W.J. Clawson. (1980). Livestock utilization of California's oak woodlands. In T. R. Plumb (Ed.), *Proceedings of the symposium on the ecology, management, and utilization of California oaks* (pp. 306-313). Berkeley: U.S. Department of Agriculture, Forest Service Pacific Southwest Forest and Range Experiment Station.

Eagleman, J. R. (1983). *Severe and unusual weather.* New York: Van Nostrand Reinhold Co.

Ebeling, W. (1986). *Handbook of Indian foods and fibers of arid America.* Berkeley: Univ. of California.

Edminster, F.C. (1954). *American game birds of field and forest: Their habits, ecology and management.* New York: Charles Scribner's Sons.

Evans, R.A. & Young, J.A. (1972). Competition within the grass community. In, V.B. Younger and C.M. McKell (Eds.), *The biology and utilization of grasses* (pp. 230-249). New York: Academic Press.

Felt, E.P. (1940). *Plant galls and gall makers.* New York: Hafner.

Fitch, H.S. (1948). Ecology of the California ground squirrel on grazing lands. *American Midland Naturalist,* **39** (3), 513-596.

Font, P. (1933). *Anza's California expeditions: Font's complete diary of the second Anza expedition* (Vol. IV). (H.E Bolton, Trans. and Ed.). Berkeley: University of California Press.

Forbush, E.H. (1939). *A natural history of American birds of eastern and central North America.* (Rev. & Abridged J.R. May). Boston: Houghton Mifflin. (Original work published 1925.)

Fox, D.L. (1976). *Animal biochromes and structural colors* (2nd ed.). Berkeley: University of California Press.

Frazer, J. (1981). *The golden bough: The roots of religion and folklore.* New York: Avenel. (Original work published 1890.)

Golde, R.H. (1973). *Lightning protection.* London: Edward Arnold.

Golde, R.H. (1977). Lightning currents and related parameters. In R.H. Golde (Ed.), *Lightning* (Vols. 1-2) (pp. 309-350). New York: Academic Press.

Goldsmith, E.E. (1973). *Ancient pagan symbols.* New York: AMS Press.

Goodwin, D. (1977). *Pigeons and doves of the world* (2nd ed.). Ithaca, NY: Cornell University Press.

Gordon, D.R., J.M. Welker, J.M. Mencke, and Rice, K.J. (1989). Neighbourhood competition between annual plants and blue oak (Quercus douglasii) seedlings. *Oecologia,* **7** (9), 533-541.

Graves, R. (1942). *The white goddess.* First American Edition, 1966. USA: International Authors.

Griffin, J.R. (1971). Oak regeneration in the upper Carmel Valley, CA. *Ecology,* **52** (5), 862-868.

Griffin, J.R. (1973). Valley oaks—the end of an era? *Fremontia,* **1** (1), 5-9.

Griffin, J.R. & W.B. Critchfield. (1976). *The distribution of forest trees in California.* Berkeley, CA: U.S. Department of Agriculture. Forest Service Pacific Southwest Forest and Range Experiment Station.

Grinnell, J. (1923). The burrowing rodents of California as agents in soil formation. *Journal of Mammalogy,* **4** (3), 137-149.

Grinnell, J., Dixon, J.S. & Linsdale, J.M. (1937). *Fur bearing mammals of California: Their natural history, systematic status, and relations to man* (Vol. 2). Berkeley: University of California Press.

Grimm, J. (1966). *Teutonic mythology* (Vols. 1-4). (J.S. Stallybrass, Trans.). New York: Dover. (Original work published 1883.)

Gruson, E.S. (1972). *Words for birds: A lexicon of North American birds with biographical notes.* New York: Quadrangle Books.

Gubernatis, A. de. (1968). *Zoological mythologies* (Vols 1-2). Detroit: Singing Press. (Original work published 1883.)

Hale, E.E. (1968). *His level best and other stories.* The American Short Stories Series, vol. 18. New York: Garrett Press. (Original work published 1872.)

Haggard, H.W. (1929). *Devils, drugs, and doctors.* New York: Harper & Brothers.

Hansen, H.A. (1976). *The witch's garden.* (Muriel Crofts, Trans.) New York: Unity Press.

Harlan, J.R. (1992). Origins and processes of domestication. In G.P. Chapman (Ed.), *Grass evolution and domestication* (pp. 159-175). Cambridge: Cambridge University Press.

Harmon, W. (Ed.) (1992). *The top 500 poems.* New York: Columbia University Press.

Hathaway, N. (1994). *The friendly guide to the universe.* New York: Penguin Books.

Hawksworth, F.G. (1983). Mistletoes as forest parasites. In Malcolm Clader & Peter Bernhardt (Eds.), *The biology of mistletoes* (pp. 317-327). North Ryde, Australia: Academic Press Australia.

Heady, H.F. and R.D. Child. (1994). *Rangeland ecology and management.* Boulder: Westview Press.

Heerwagen, J.H. & Orians, G.H. (1993). Humans, habitats, and aesthetics. In Stephen R. Kellert & Edward O. Wilson (Eds.), *The biophilia hypothesis* (pp. 138-172). Washington, D.C.: Island Press.

Heiser, C.B. (1969). *Nightshades: The paradoxical plants.* San Francisco: W.H. Freeman.

Hehn, V. & Stallybrass, J.S. (1888). *The wanderings of plants and animals from their first home.* London: Swan Sonnenschien.

Hendry, G.W. (1931). The adobe brick as a historical source. *Agricultural History, 5* (3), 110-127.

Hittell, T.H. (1885). *History of California* (Vols. 1-2). San Francisco: Pacific Press and Occidental.

Holland, V.L. (1973). *A study of soil and vegetation under Quercus douglasii H. & A. compared to open grassland.* Berkeley: University of California. 369 pp. Dissertation.

Holland, V.L. (1976). In defense of blue oaks. *Fremontia, 4* (1), 3-8.

Holland, V.L. (1980). Effect of blue oak on rangeland forage production in central California. In T. R. Plumb (Ed.), *Proceedings of the symposium on the ecology, management, and utilization of California oaks* (pp. 314-318). Berkeley: U.S. Department of Agriculture, Forest Service Pacific Southwest Forest and Range Experiment Station.

Holland, V.L. & J. Morton. (1980). Effect of blue oak on nutritional quality of rangeland forage in central California. In T. R. Plumb (Ed.), *Proceedings of the symposium on the ecology, management, and utilization of California oaks* (pp. 319-322). Berkeley: U.S. Department of Agriculture, Forest Service Pacific Southwest Forest and Range Experiment Station.

Holy bible. King James Version.

Inglis, B. (1965). *A history of medicine.* Cleveland: World Publishing.

Jacobs, D. (1965). *A witches guide to gardening.* New York: Taplinger.

Jacobs, D. (1967). *Cures and curses.* 1967. London: Elek.

Jain, S.K. 1972. Population interactions, diversity, and community structure. In V.B. Younger and C.M. McKell (Eds.), *The biology and utilization of grasses* (pp. 212-229). New York: Academic Press.

Jepson, W.L. (1910). *The silva of California.* Berkeley: University Press.

Johnson, E.V. (1984, Spring). Lecture series prsented in *Ornithology,* California Polytechnic University, San Luis Obispo.

Kelley, W.K. (1969). Curiosities of Indo-European tradition and folklore. Detroit: Singing Tree Press. (Original work published 1863.)

Kingsbury, J.M. (1965). *Deadly harvest: A guide to common poisonous plants.* New York: Holt, Rinehart and Winston.

Kroeber, A.L. (1925). *Handbook of the Indians of California.* Berkeley: University of California Press.

Kuhn-Schnyder, E. & H. Rieber. (1986). *Handbook of paleozoology* (Trans., Emil Kucera). Baltimore: John Hopkins University Press.

Kurten, B. & Anderson, E. (1980). *Pleistocene mammals of North America.* New York: Columbia University Press.

Langston, R.L. & Powell, J.A. (1975). The earwigs of California (order Dermaptera) (Vol. 20) *Bulletin of the California Insect Survey.* Berkeley: University of California Press.

Lao-tzu. (1955). *The way of life.* (Trans. Raymond B. Blakney). New York: Mentor.

Lao-tzu. (1985). *The way of Lao Tzu (Tao-te ching).* (Trans. Wing-tsit Chan.) New York: Macmillan.

Laughrin, L. (1970). *San Joaquin kit fox, its distribution and abundance.* State of California, Dept. of Fish and Game. Wildlife Management Branch Administrative Rep No. 70-2. 19pp.

Lawrence, E.A. (1993). The sacred bee, the filthy pig, and the bat out of hell: Animal symbolism as cognitive biophilia. In Stephen R. Kellert & Edward O. Wilson (Eds.), *The biophilia hypothesis* (pp. 301-344). Washington, D.C.: Island Press.

le Strange, R. (1977). *A history of herbal plants.* London: Angus & Robertson.

Leach, M. (Ed.) (1950). *Funk and Wagnalls standard dictionary of folklore, mythology and legend* (Vols. 1-2) New York: Funk and Wagnalls Co.

Lee, W.R. (1977). Lightning injuries and death. In R.H. Golde (Ed.), *Lightning* (Vols. 1-2) (pp. 521-543) New York: Academic Press.

Leopold, A. (1948). *Game management*. New York: Charles Scribners.

Levi, W.M. (1957). *The pigeon* (3rd ed.). Sumter: W.M.

Linsdale, J.M. (1937). *The natural history of magpies*. Pacific Coast Avifauna, No. 25. Berkeley: Cooper Ornithological Club.

Linsdale, J.M. (1946). *The California ground squirrel: A record of observations made on the Hastings Nature Reservation*. Berkeley: University of California Press.

Logan, C.G., W.H. Berry, W.G. Standley and T.T. Kato. (1992). *Prey abundance and food habits of San Joaquin kit fox* (Vulpes velox macrotis) *at Camp Roberts Army National Guard Training Site, California*. U.S. Department of Energy Topical Report, EG&G/EM Santa Barbara Operations Report No. EGG10617-2158. 21pp.

Lum, P. (1948). *The stars in our heavens: Myths and fables*. New York: Pantheon.

Lumsden, C.J. and E.O. Wilson. (1981). *Genes, mind, and culture*. Cambridge: Harvard University Press.

Lumsden, C.J. and E.O. Wilson. (1983). *Promethean fire: Reflections on the origin of mind*. Cambridge: Harvard University Press.

Lundelius, E.L. Jr., Graham, R.W. Anderson, E., Guilday, J., Holman, J.A., Steadman, D.W. and S.D. Webb. (1983). Terrestrial vertebrate faunas. In S.C. Porter (Ed.), *Late quarternary environments of the United States* (Vol. 1) (pp. 311-353). Minneapolis: University of Minnesota.

MacCana, P. (1970). *Celtic mythology*. Feltham: Hamlyn.

MacCulloch, J.A. (1911). *The religion of the ancient Celts*. Edinburgh: T. & T. Clark.

MacRoberts, M.H. (1970). Notes on the food habits and food defense of the acorn woodpecker. *Condor*, **72**, pp. 196-204.

MacRoberts, M.H. (1974). Acorns, woodpeckers, grubs and scientists. *Pacific Discovery*, **27** (5), pp. 9-15.

Maeterlinck, M. (1929). *The blue bird: A fairy play in six acts* (A.T. de Mattos, Trans.). New York: Dodd, Mead. (Original work published 1907.)

Mallette, R.D. (1987). *Upland game of California* (4th ed.). Sacramento: Department of Fish and Game.

Marshall, J.L. (1983). *Lightning protection*. New York: John Wiley & Sons.

May, P.R.A., Fuster, J.A., Newman, P. and Hirschman, A. (1976). Woodpeckers and head injury. *Lancet*, **1**, 454-455.

Mayer, P.J. (1976). *Miwok balanophagy: Implications for the cultural development of some California acorn-eaters.* Berkeley: University of California Press.

McCulloch, F. (1962). *Medieval Latin and French bestiaries.* Chapel Hill: University of North Carolina Press.

Mercure, A., K. Ralls, K.P. Koepfli, & Wayne, R.K. (1993). Genetic subdivisions among small canids: Mitochondrial DNA differentiation of swift, kit, and arctic foxes. *Evolution, 47* (5), 1313-1328.

Merriam, C. Hart. (1918). The acorn, a possibly neglected source of food. *National Geographic Magazine, 34,* 129-137.

Metropolitan Museum of Art, New York. (1965). *A cloisters bestiary.* New York: Metropolitan Museum of Art.

Miles, C.A. (1976). *Christmas customs and traditions: Their history and significance.* New York: Dover. (Original work published 1912.)

Miller, A.H. (1932). The fossil passerine birds from the Pleistocene of Carpinteria, California. *Bulletin of Geological Science, 21,* 169-194.

Miller, A.H. (1937). Biotic associations and life-zones in relation to the Pleistocene birds of California. *Condor, 39,* 248-252.

Moore, J. A. (1993). *Science as a way of knowing: The foundations of modern biology.* London and Cambridge: Harvard University Press.

Moore, M. (1979). *Medicinal plants of the mountain west.* Santa Fe: Museum of New Mexico.

Muick, P. & J. Stewart. (1992) (3rd ed.) *Oak action kit: resources for preservation and conservation of oak habitats.* Sacramento: California Native Plant Society.

Nelson, R. (1993). Searching for the lost arrow: Physical and spiritual ecology in the hunter's world. In Stephen R. Kellert & Edward O. Wilson (Eds.), *The biophilia hypothesis* (pp. 201-228). Washington, D.C.: Island Press.

O'Farrell, T.P. (1987). Kit fox. In M. Novak, J.A. Baker, M.E. Obbard and B. Malloch (Eds.), *Wild furbearer management and conservation in North America* (pp. 422-431). Ontario, Canada: Ministry of Natural Resources.

Orloff, S., F. Hall and L. Spiegel. (1986). Distribution and habitat requirements of the San Joaquin kit fox in the northern extreme of their range. *Transactions of the Western Section Wildlife Society, 22,* 60-70.

Osol, A., Pratt, R. & Gennaro, A.R. (Eds.). (1973). *The United States dispensatory.* (27th ed.). Philadelphia: J.B. Lippincott.

Ovid. (1955). *Metamorphoses*. (M.M. Innes, Trans.). London: Penguin Press. (Original work published 1 BC.)

Oxford English Dictionary. (1961). Oxford: Clarendon Press.

Palou, F. (1926). *Historical memoirs of New California* (Vol. II). (H.E Bolton, Trans. and Ed.). New York: Russell & Russell.

Pavlik, B. (1991). *Oaks of California*. Los Olivos, California: Cachuma Press.

Pearson, T. G. (Ed.). (1936). *Birds of America*. New York: Doubleday.

Physiologus. (1979). (M.J. Curley, Trans.) (Original work published circa 300 AD.)

Pliny the Elder. (1967). *Natural history* (Vols. 1-6). (H. Rackam and W. H. S. Jones, Trans. and Eds.). London: H.G. Bohn. (Original work published circa 300 BC.)

Porteous, A. (1968). *Forest folklore, mythology, and romance*. Detroit: Singing Tree Press. (Original work published 1928.)

Proctor, P.M. (1972). *Star myths and stories: From Andromeda to Virgo*. New York: Exposition Press.

Reynolds, M.D. (1995). Yellow-billed magpie (*Pica nuttalli*). In A. Poole & F. Gill (Eds.), *The birds of North America, No. 180*. Philadelphia: Academy of Natural Sciences.

Richman, I.B. (1965). *California under Spain and Mexico, 1535-1847*. New York: Cooper Square.

Richardson, M. (1972). *The fascination of reptiles*. New York: Hill and Wang.

Ritter, W.E. (1938). *The California woodpecker and I*. Berkeley: University of California Press.

Roberts, S.W. & R.L. Smith. (1980). Aspects of water relations in coast live oaks and valley oaks subjected to root damage from land development operations. In T. R. Plumb (Ed.) *Proceedings of the symposium on the ecology, management, and utilization of California oaks* (pp. 171-175). Berkeley: U.S. Department of Agriculture, Forest Service Pacific Southwest Forest and Range Experiment Station.

Robbins, C.S., B. Bruun and H.S. Zim. (1983). *Birds of North America*. New York: Golden Press.

Robbins, C.T., S. Mole, A.E. Hagerman, & T.A. Hanley. (1987a). Role of tannins in defending plants against ruminants: Reduction in dry matter digestion. *Ecology,* **68** (6), 1606-1615.

Robbins, C.T., T.A. Hanley, A.E. Hagerman, O. Hjeljord, D.L. Baker, C.C. Schwartz & W.W. Mautz. (1987b). Role of tannins in defending plants against ruminants: Reduction in protein availability. *Ecology, 68* (1), 98-107.

Ross, A. (1967). *Pagan Celtic Britain: Studies in iconography and tradition.* New York: Columbia University Press.

Rossi, (1979). *Land use and vegetation change in the oak woodland-savanna of northern San Luis Obispo County, CA.* Berkeley: University of California. 337 p. Dissertation.

Rossi, R.S. (1980). History of cultural influences on the distribution and reproduction of oaks in California. In T. R. Plumb (Ed.), *Proceedings of the symposium on the ecology, management, and utilization of California oaks* (pp. 7-18). Berkeley: U.S. Department of Agriculture, Forest Service Pacific Southwest Forest and Range Experiment Station.

Rowland, B. (1978). *Birds with human souls.* Knoxville: University of Tennessee Press.

Rowland, B. (1989). The art of memory and the bestiary. In W.B. Clark and M.T. McMunn (Eds.), *Beasts and birds of the Middle Ages: The bestiary and its legacy* (pp. 12-25). Philadelphia: University of Pennsylvania Press.

Russo, R.A. (1979). *Plant galls of the California region.* Pacific Grove: Boxwood Press.

Sarton, G. (1927). *Introduction to the history of science: From Homer to Omar Khayyam* (Vol. 1). Baltimore: The Williams and Wilkins Co.

Sarton, G. (1952). *A history of science: Ancient science through the golden age of Greece.* Cambridge: Harvard University Press.

Sauer, J.D. (1993). *Historical geography of crop plants: A select roster.* Boca Raton: CRC Press.

Schitoskey, F., Jr. (1973). *Energy requirements and diet of the California ground squirrel, Spermophilus beecheyi* (Doctoral dissertation, University of California at Davis, 1973).

Schleiffer, H. (1973). *Sacred narcotic plants of the New World Indians.* New York: Hafner Press.

Schleiffer, H. (1979). *Narcotic plants of the Old World.* Monticello: Lubrecht & Cramer.

Schoenherr, A.A. (1992). *A natural history of California.* Berkeley: University of California Press.

Schonland, B. F. J.(1964). *The flight of thunderbolts.* Oxford: Clarendon Press.

Schorger, A.W. (1955). *The passenger pigeon: Its natural history and extinction.* Madison: University of Wisconsin Press.

Schultes, R.E. (1979). Solanaceous hallucinogens in the New World. In J.G. Hawkes, R.N. Lester & A.D. Skelding (Eds.), *The biology and taxonomy of the Solanaceae* (pp. 137-160). London: Academic Press.

Schultes, R.E., & Hofmann, A. (1973). *The botany and chemistry of hallucinogens.* Springfield: Charles C. Thomas.

Seligmann, K. (1948). *The history of magic.* New York: Pantheon.

Siegel, R. K. (1984). The natural history of hallucinogens. In B.L. Jacobs (Ed.), *Hallucinogens: Neurochemical, behavioral, and clinical perspectives* (pp. 1-18). New York: Raven Press.

Simon, H. (1971). *The splendor of iridescence: Structural colors in the animal world.* New York: Dodd, Mead.

Simons, D.D. (1983). Interactions between California condors and humans in prehistoric far western North America. In S.R. Wilbur and J.A. Jackson (Eds.), *Vulture biology and management* (pp. 470-494). Berkeley: University of California Press.

Singer, C.J. (1958). *From magic to science.* New York: Dover. (Original work published 1958.)

Smith, E.R. (1980). *The California ground squirrel* (Spermophilus beecheyi) *natural history and control policies with economic and ecological ramifications.* San Francisco: San Francisco State Univ. Master's thesis.

Smith, H.M. (1946). *Handbook of lizards: Lizards of the United States and of Canada.* New York: Comstock.

Smith, W.A. (1968). The band tailed pigeon in California. *California Fish and Game,* **54** (1), 4-16.

Spence, L. 1971. *The history and origins of Druidism.* New York: Samuel Weiser.

Spencer, E.R. (1957). *Just weeds.* New York: Charles Scribner's Sons.

Steinbeck, J. (1975). *To a god unknown.* London: Pan Books. (Originally published 1935.)

Steinbeck, J. (1952). *East of Eden.* New York: Viking Press.

Swann, H.K. (1968). *A dictionary of English and folk-names of British birds.* Detroit: Gale Research. (Original work published 1913.)

Taylor, A.R. (1977). Lightning and trees. In R.H. Golde (Ed.), *Lightning* (Vols 1-2) (pp. 831-849). New York: Academic Press.

Taylor, N. (1965). *Plant drugs that changed the world*. New York: Dodd, Mead & Co.

Thiselton-Dyer, T. F. (1968). *The folk-lore of plants*. Detroit: Singing Tree Press. (Original work published 1889.)

Thiselton-Dyer, T.F. (1971). *English folk-lore: A facsimile of the first edition*. Ann Arbor: Gryphon. (Original work published 1878.)

Topsell, E. (1967). *The history of four-footed beasts and serpents and insects* (Vol. 1). (Introd. Willy Ley). New York: Da Capo Press. (Original work published in 1658.)

Torrey, B. (1913). *Field-days in California*. New York: Houghton Mifflin.

Toynbee, J.M.C. (1973). *Animals in Roman life and art*. New York: Cornell University Press.

Tucker, J.M. (1980). Taxonomy of California oaks. In T. R. Plumb (Ed.), *Proceedings of the symposium on the ecology, management, and utilization of California oaks* (pp. 19-29). Berkeley: U.S. Department of Agriculture, Forest Service Pacific Southwest Forest and Range Experiment Station.

Ulrich, R.S. (1993). Biophilia, biophobia, and natural landscapes. In Stephen R. Kellert & Edward O. Wilson (Eds.), *The biophilia hypothesis* (pp. 73-137). Washington, D.C.: Island Press.

Uman, M.A. (1987). *The lightning discharge*. Orlando: Academic Press.

Waters, J.H. (1964). Red fox and gray fox from New England archeological sites. *Journal of Mammalogy, 45,* 307-308.

Weather Service Headquarters. (1993). *A summary of natural hazard deaths for 1991 in the United States*. Silver Springs: Warning and Forecast Branch, Weather Service Headquarters.

Webb, E.J. (1952). *The names of the stars*. London: Nisbet.

Weld, L.H. (1957). *Cynipid galls of the Pacific Slope*. Ann Arbor: privately printed.

Welty, J.C. & L. Baptista. (1988). *The life of birds* (4th ed.). New York: W.B. Saunders.

Wheelock, I.G. (1913). *Birds of California: An introduction to more than three hundred common birds of the state and adjacent islands*. (4th ed.). Chicago: McClurg & Co.

White, T.H. (1954). *The book of beasts: Being a translation from a Latin bestiary of the twelfth century.* New York: Putnam.

Wiebes-Rijks, A.A. & Shorthouse, J.D. (1992). Ecological relationships of insects inhabiting Cynipid galls. In Joseph D. Shorthouse & Odette Rohfritsch (Eds.), *Biology of insect-induced galls* (pp. 238-257). New York: Oxford Press.

Wilson, E.O. (1984). *Biophilia.* Cambridge, MA: Harvard University Press.

Wilson, E.O. (1993). Biophilia and the conservation ethic. In Stephen R. Kellert & Edward O. Wilson (Eds.), *The biophilia hypothesis* (pp. 31-41). Washington, D.C.: Island Press.

Winkler, H., Christie, D.A. & D. Nurney. (1995). *Woodpeckers: A guide to the woodpeckers of the world.* Boston: Houghton Mifflin.

World Almanac Book of Facts. (1997). Mahwah, NJ: World Almanac Books.

Zohary, D. & Hopf, M. (1993). *Domestication of plants in the Old World: The origin and spread of cultivated plants in West Asia, Europe, and the Nile Valley* (2nd ed.). Oxford: Clarendon Press.

Index

About the Author

Baxter Trautman grew up in Latin America and upstate New York. She received her master's degree in biology from California State University at San Luis Obispo and wrote her master's thesis on the mythology and science of California's coastal grasslands–the theme of this book. She lives in Pozo, California, a town of fifty people near San Luis Obispo.